Preoccupied with Promise

Reclaim the Contagious Joy
You Were Meant to Experience Now

Courtney J. Strong

randall house

114 Bush Rd I Nashville, TN 37217
randallhouse.com

Printed in the United States of America

ISBN-13:9780892659739

For

Hunter
My dear friend, fellow author, and disciple of Christ

and

Paisley
My spunky pal and partner (already) in women's ministry

Contents

Introduction vii

Week 1 Lead Role on a Hollywood Set 1

Week 2 Defensive Strategies for a Well-Accessorized Mind 27

Week 3 Specific Gifts You Can Know 53

Week 4 Every Girl Loves a S.A.L.E. 85

Week 5 For You to Experience 109

Week 6 End With a Twirl 137

Conclusion 167

Acknowledgements 169

Note to Leaders 173

Engraving Questions 175

Endnotes 177

Introduction

Friend,

As I write this Bible study, I'm sitting at my hometown coffee shop, surrounded by the locals picking up their brewed afternoon treats. A dad takes his preteen out for an end-of-summer drink. Meetings happen over mugs. You can spot the regulars a mile away . . . or can you? There are no frowns. No smiles. People are just *there*. Everyone seems to wander in faithfully like it's a routine, luxurious chore. Journeying to that familiar counter and retrieving their daily cups.

Customers come for all different reasons—a quick stop before work, a conversation, a business deal. But there's one undeniable common denominator that coffee shops count on to keep them in the black: the customer needs to come back. The appetite is not fed all week or even all day on a grande.

It's the modern-day water well.

In the story of Jesus and the woman at the water well, He promised He could end the repetition in her life. He appealed to her daily routine when he said, "Anyone who drinks this water will soon become thirsty again. But those who drink the water I give will never be thirsty again. It becomes a fresh, bubbling spring within them, giving them eternal life" (John 4:13-14, NLT).

Ahh! But we are so far from this image! Sometimes I feel like my life more closely resembles flat, left-over-from-the-last-birthday-party, three-month-old soda. The good news is that this isn't all there is; there's more God intends for us. We aren't meant for motionless, stagnant water. We were meant for vibrancy, for joy—for a *stirring*. A life of anticipation, not monotony, awaits us.

There's another piece of good news. We're going to do this by exercising a pattern women are already experts at: thinking, re-thinking, and letting our thoughts linger in our heads. Truly, ladies, we are already really good at this! How many times do we act on this in a negative sense? We hash out a whole situation in our heads in a split second, well before anything becomes reality, and we don't let it go. But now, we have the opportunity to turn our thoughts around and use this habit for our win! Thank You, Jesus! Together we will learn a different way to daydream. We will learn this truth—if our minds have the ability to be engrossed with problems, they also have the capacity to be preoccupied with promise.

This workbook includes six weeks of study. Each week consists of five days of Bible study experience. Friends, the days will differ in length. Especially at the beginning as we get our gears turning—push with me through some of our foundational work—and you'll be so glad you did. Take comfort that another reason the length will seem to differ for everyone, beyond setting the foundation, is because God is going to make this very personal for you. Some concepts your heart will need to spend more time on, and you will need less time on others. Let those moments happen. And if we're real with one another, we know of many other things that can influence the amount of time we set aside for this. With regard to babies waking up earlier than normal in the morning and alarms not going off and any other thing that might interfere with your "length" of study . . . we're just going to pray against those and smile, knowing we are all dealing with similar struggles but have a victorious God—the One who sees us, *El Roi* (Gen. 16:13-14)—at our side.

Materials needed:

- Workbook
- Bible
- Pen
- Highlighter, marker, or pen of a different color to mark text that is meaningful to you

Nightlights:

The workbook is intended for brief study with all-day focus. Some lessons contain an application question for the end of the day to reinforce what you've learned. These are labeled as **"Nightlights"**— single question wrap-ups peppered throughout the study. You'll notice these become more consistent in later weeks to hopefully start a habit of thinking about what we learned throughout the day. I believe God will do great work through these follow-up questions, as we commit to make this an on-going lifestyle that does not start and stop with the opening and closing of a physical workbook. This really can become a pulse in your mind that *lasts*. As my pastor, Gregg Matte, puts it, "I tune my instrument in the morning, and review the songs we sang all day in the evening." He believes, *"If I do both [morning and night], I'll grow in the Lord twice as fast!"*

Engraving Questions:

I recently took my charm bracelet to a jeweler to add about seven trinkets dear to my heart. Cherished as they were, it took years before they made it to the sautering stage. The night I picked up my "new" bracelet, I stayed in the car with the kids while we dropped my husband off to run a quick errand. Up until this moment, the bracelet and all its charms served only to entertain me. Glancing in the backseat, I saw a stack of read and re-read books, a television screen I did not want to turn on, and eager eyes pleading to "do something fun." I began to show them my bracelet. The stories naturally unfolded. I relished the moments as my son and daughter took turns asking me about the different meaning for each charm.

Just like gems on our bracelet, I believe the Lord wants to collect our impressionable moments in one place for reference. First for our heart. Some of them *solely* for our heart. Other stories we will have the joy of sharing.

Within each week in our study, one main question is highlighted as an overarching, important idea or thought labeled "Engraving Question." My hope is that these words from the Lord will reach beyond words on a page, beyond a quick second in your ears. The Lord wants these *etched on your heart*. I picture the two of you sitting in a chair with a scrapbook, looking through lessons learned as He gently guides your hand over the pages, pointing out important moments. On those days when this world is hard and you cannot see, when tears cloud your eyes or doubting fogs your faith, your fingertips will find truth in the etchings, His promises you committed to knowing.

These special questions and answers are to be re-recorded in a reserved spot at the very end of the study, so you will have all your major learning points in one place. Use this as your own personal charm bracelet, etched on your heart with the finest craftsmanship from the Holy Spirit with unique stories you'll be excited to share with others.

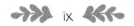

My son is really into the "superhero" phase. If I could pick a super power, one of my top choices would be the ability to be in two places at once. I'd specifically enjoy being able to be with each of you as you go on this journey. I would love to share the happiness in your room—whatever room you happen to be in—when you find out the truth your heart has been longing to hear. I would love to sit across from you and see the pleasant relief on your face, as if you had opened an awaited present while you make truth discoveries in these six weeks. Yes, I wish I could witness that moment between you and the Lord, but I'll just let the two of you enjoy the experience together.

Now . . .

Picture an easel, covered with a dreamy blue velvet tapestry. Someone who loves you dearly is about to dramatically disclose what's behind it.

True story. And it happens to be the theme backdrop for our study.

Let's get started.

Lead Role on a Hollywood Set

Week 1 — Day One

We all read stories with silent questions dancing around in our heads. While our eyes physically read left to right on the page, our hearts are searching all around the 12-point font for a magnet of connection. We long to see a place where we identify with a character. Where we see ourselves in the story. Where we have an "aha" moment, a sigh of relief to know we aren't the only one who feels that way. We long to see similar happiness we've known and the rain-soaked paths of grief we've travelled. Beyond that, we'll hope to see our characters show us how to continue in joy and further still, emerge in faith *against* all hope after the hard seasons of "life" touched them.

The purpose of this study is to pose and answer this question: "What if you could experience freedom and a welling up of enthusiasm even after you experienced 'life'?" Can a person really go from stale to stirred?

To that, I'd say—show me someone who has lived life, the good and the bad, and returned to an enthusiastic, child-like heart. It's desired, but hard to picture. A real story. A non-fiction person. And not someone who has a story modified for the social media feed. *Show me.* Because maybe you are like me, and you so badly want to believe this could be true.

A glimpse of our hope is found in John 4.

Before reading our text for today, write down the first ideas that come to mind when you think of the woman at the well. If you don't have any preconceptions, don't worry—we're about to learn a lot together!

Read the first part of our story in John 4:1-9.

As our story begins, we're dropped right beside the woman in the middle of her daily grind. It probably held every characteristic of a Monday. When we meet her, she is caught up in routine. We can already identify with this girl. She's completing a necessary, rigorous chore.

Let's dive into a couple of facts that give the setting of this true story a unique twist. Tenney's commentary suggests the woman arrived at the well close to noon. In the heat of the day is a strange time for the woman to retrieve water.[1] It's highly possible she did not want to face the judgment of other townspeople, as her lifestyle resembled a modern day reality television show, popular only because of the compounding scandals (more about this later). It seems she wanted to be alone, but she probably really didn't (you know how we females are complicated creatures).

When she reached the well—tired, out of breath and sweaty—she found a mysterious man whom she thought messed up her plan of having some alone time. And it wasn't just another man from her Samaritan community. It was a Jew. This was a big deal. We get long standing rivalry, but this is beyond Longhorns versus Aggies; actual hatred existed between these two people groups.[2] And the awkward moments had only just begun. Not only was this Jewish man in her company, He also spoke with her, and then asked her for a drink *from a Samaritan cup.*

Often we think God is taking something from us when He's actually on the brink of handing us a blessing. Have you ever experienced this feeling? Record two or three examples of something God has asked of you and the blessings He was trying to accomplish or the blessing He was trying to give.

Something He's asked of me: **The blessing He was trying to give:**

Keep up the discovery by reading verses 10-15 of chapter 4.

In verse 15, the woman gives an "Absolutely!" to this man who offered her living water. Why? So she won't have to keep coming here to draw water.

What is one thing you wish you didn't have to "keep coming back to do time and again"?

What about your thought life? Is there a doubt or fear you "keep coming back to" but desire to rid it from your mind? List it here.

What do you believe Jesus has to say to you about this? Read James 4:7-8 and Romans 12:1-2 for additional clues.

I believe one thing Jesus is saying: "I long to renew you regarding these things."

Let's continue in the text: Things are about to get awkward! Read John 4:16-18 (provided below):

"Go call your husband," He told her, "and come back here."

"I don't have a husband," she answered.

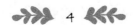

"You have correctly said, 'I don't have a husband,' " Jesus said. "For you've had five husbands, and the man you now have is not your husband. What you have said is true."

Before He continues, Jesus asks the woman to bring her husband into the conversation. This was not an unusual request, as it was proper to invite a woman's husband into the situation if a man and woman were talking one-on-one.[3] When Jesus addresses her marital status, we learn about the woman's past.

This relational history is where we get the idea that she was at the well at noon to avoid the cruelty and the deliberate isolation because of her reputation. This is also where I've learned of possibly a different, very interesting side to the story. What if she was avoiding the well for another reason?

Remember, at the beginning of today's lesson, we listed our first thoughts when we hear about the woman at the well. For years, I thought the Samaritan woman's narrative pointed to a promiscuous woman who found beautiful forgiveness. Her story is often told, and rightfully so, to demonstrate how Jesus exchanges our shame for dignity. I want to challenge us to think that her past relationships were not the only theme of her story.

A first century Judean scholar provides information that it was more likely that her relationship issues (male and then subsequently, female) were because she was *barren*.[4] Let that soak in. Barren. Yes. Can you believe it? My soul hushed as I discovered this. Maybe the townspeople were still gossiping about her many marriages, but the scholar suggests that the fact she could not have children was the reason *why* she married so many times. Upon finding out she could not have children, each man left. This sends my head spinning with unique insight into her longing. It's no wonder about her excitement. *Jesus' offer of something living inside of her was hope no one—no one—had ever given her.* She's more like us today than perhaps we ever thought.

In what ways do you understand what the Samaritan woman might have felt here?

Take another look at verse 14. The New Living Translation says, "But those who drink the water I give will never be thirsty again. It becomes a fresh, bubbling spring within them, giving them eternal life."

What words stand out to you in this verse?

In what way do they bring meaning to you personally?

I find it interesting (and actually love) that the New Living Translation uses the word "bubbling" to describe the water Jesus wanted to give. The concept must have sounded foreign to the woman who may have had the mentality of "it is what it is" about her place in this world. Picture again the flat, left-over-from-the-last-birthday-party, three-month-old soda.

As females, we get a bad reputation for our love of drama. A bad reputation is actually appropriate when it involves gossip. However, our affinity for drama in its purest form originates in our preference for movement, for situations and seasons to change, for life to take the twists it naturally begs for. The word picture God gives us here in verse 14 reminds us there is movement when we feel like there is none.

The Lord showed me another reason why the woman's promiscuity was not the focus. Not that it was all right that she was living with a man to whom she was not married. Not that the Lord dismisses some unrighteousness and disciplines others. But in this case, don't you find it interesting that the focus of His dialogue with her was not about forgiveness, but about giving His gift of life? In John 8, we find Jesus speaking to another adulterous woman. Jesus was not condemning this woman either (that was the Pharisees' hobby); however, Jesus' words to her were about forgiveness of sin. Jesus' focus on the woman at the well was a filling of the void in her life. No empty place can be filled without Jesus' forgiveness, yet when He approached this woman about her salvation, He extended it through such a tangible, personal need.

Whatever areas in your life feel stale, He can revive them. And not just recover to sit on the shelf again. We don't magnify God in our thoughts when we think of His revitalization as something barely giving us a limp-along pulse. No, this is much more. His love will stir it to the bubbling point. If we only knew . . . may we decide together with the Spirit that we *will know.*

Conclude today by reading Romans 4:17.

". . . He [Abraham] believed in God, who gives life to the dead and calls things into existence that do not exist."

What does this tell you about what God is able to do?

In what area of your life does this offer hope?

Nightlight (for tonight before you go to sleep)

Read John 4:14:

> "But those who drink the water I give will never be thirsty again. It becomes a fresh, bubbling spring within them, giving them eternal life" (NLT).

Re-read your thoughts journaled about Romans 4:17 at the end of today's lesson. Goodnight. God has good things in store!

Week 1 Day Two

I've diagnosed myself with cinema spectator empathy. It's the insatiable urge to tell Annie her parents are liars so she feels the freedom to live with Mr. Warbucks or to let the charming maiden of Green Gables know Gilbert Blythe is actually quite fond of her and genuinely sorry for his "Carrots" insult.

These symptoms are exactly what Hollywood wants us to experience. The industry thrives on pulling at the audience's emotional heartstrings. The producers accomplish this by showing both scenes to the audience, while the protagonist is only aware of the story-line from his or her point of view. The film flips back and forth between the simultaneous experiences of the lead role, the hero, the villain, and the helpful friend. Admittedly, the tension is what makes a movie interesting, and to deliver the redeeming, pivotal piece of information too early would not sell a blockbuster. Still, the whole time I watch the movie, something inside me groans for the main characters to know what they do not.

It is important to note the empathy element of the movie experience. Empathy is emotionally imagining oneself in someone else's shoes. On a deeper level, perhaps this angle engages us because we see a little bit of ourselves in the characters who lack information. We feel a fear almost too close to home: *we see the main character missing out on something.*

What makes the climax of the story even more gut-wrenching are those five little words at the beginning of a film: BASED ON A TRUE STORY. And with the woman at the well, this, my friends, is what we have.

Simultaneous scenes surround this true story of the woman at the well. Imagine with me. Perhaps the night before her journey, the woman struggled to go to sleep, her complexion moistened with tears. Now switch scenes. We see Jesus intentionally leaving Judea, making his way to meet her in Samaria. If this were made into a movie and we were the spectators, we would pull for her to hang on, to know her hope was on its way. Obviously, the first scene described here is just an imaginative assumption. However, we do know the woman had a deep emotional need, and Jesus planned this trip before she was even born.

Return to the interesting place we left off yesterday (John 4:16-18). Going further, read verses 19-25. While it is typical for a plot to portray the protagonist as blinded from some major truth, in the next verse we find out the female lead of our story *was* aware of some aspects of the plan of salvation; she was not completely void of information.

Since she was not totally clueless, what were some of the things she already knew?

1.

2.

3.

After Jesus spoke of worshipping in spirit and truth, I think all of heaven held its breath as the woman stated, "I know that Messiah (called Christ) is coming. When he comes, he will explain everything to us" (v. 25 NIV).

If she thought Jesus' prophetic knowledge about her past was intriguing, she hadn't seen anything yet. I want to stop a minute before we go on to verse 26. When my sister planned her wedding, she heard of a fellow new bride who inserted an additional song right before the bridal procession. On the program, it read "Song of Anticipation." As if the room was not already filled to capacity with excitement, with this tradition, before the bride walks down the aisle, a few more moments are given to the audience (and especially the groom) to exaggerate the thrill of the main man meeting his bride for the first time. Between verses 25 and 26, I believe we can insert a holy "Song of Anticipation" right here.

I believe Jesus was almost unable to hold back a smile as He replied to her comment.

"I, the one speaking to you—I am he"(v. 26, NIV).

This is the part in the movie you want to watch and rewind to watch again. Personally, I'm hoping for a reenactment in Heaven.

Return to verses 23 and 24, the dialogue that occurred just before this great moment.

How did Jesus say the Father wants us to worship Him?

in _____ *and in* _____

    According to *The Complete Word Study Dictionary: New Testament,* one of the Greek translations of the word *truth* used in verse 24 is "unveiled reality."[5]

In what way can you think this was truly "unveiled reality" for the Samaritan woman?

What would your life of worship look like if it were lived in "unveiled reality?"

    As we study Jesus' great reveal and we see Him "throw back the curtain," so to speak for this woman, I am reminded of another time He moved a curtain in an even more dramatic fashion.

    Read Matthew 27:50-51 and record your thoughts.

What does it look like to live in unveiled reality in light of this passage from Matthew?

Is it just me, or does something in you just want to insert a hashtag right here? C'mon, what would you put here in response to what we've studied so far today?

Read 2 Corinthians 3:12-18. I encourage you to highlight, underline, and circle along the way. Ladies, this is good stuff! Write verses 15-17 in the space below:

Because of the sacrifice of Christ, we have the privilege of living in the era of unveiled reality. Let that sink in. What joy!

Week 1   Day Three

What an exciting day we had yesterday! Let's refocus by returning to verses 25 and 26 of John 4.

"The woman said, to Him, 'I know that Messiah is coming' (who is called Christ). 'When He comes, He will explain everything to us.'

"I am He," Jesus told her, "the One speaking to you."

The milliseconds between these verses are the heart-pounding moments I'll never get over no matter how many times I read the story. It's awesome to hear the pinnacle of this story. But there's also a message for us in this.

We have something to look forward to.
We can live in anticipation.

This is huge. We all have a universal need for something to anticipate. It keeps us going. Because we know the end of the story, we get to be right there, on the brink of Jesus' great reveal, but with great hope. We get to sit at the vantage point of verse 25, with our eyes brimmed with promise because we know verse 26. We are to be totally sure and dead set on believing in that next verse.

The anticipation is exciting because we know the rest of the story. The wonder of verses 25 and 26 can be summed up in something my daughter said recently, "Surprises are fun—but really fun when you see them." BINGO.

And it's not just a one-time thing. Every day, we have an open invitation to live in this captivating spot to learn more and more about Him and to ask the Spirit to make us increasingly aware of His presence. As we are invited to live in unveiled reality, we can join in the rhythmic cycle of anticipation and sweet revelation because we know the Giver.

Name a time when having something to look forward to changed your perspective.

What does it mean for you to know this truth we are learning today—that you have something to look forward to?

Yes, we live in the era of unveiled reality. Unlike the Samaritan woman, we know the wonder that was hidden from her for a moment. But do we live like we know? Is there more we could fully know?

I want to be clear. I'm not promoting an addiction to excitement or a life lived only for the next "thrill." 1 Timothy 6:6 says, "But godliness with contentment is a great gain." Doesn't this suggest, as my pastor often says, "If God never gave us another thing, He's already given us more than enough?" Yes. Does this suggest we should be content with what we have? Yes. But that's just it. We aren't aware of all we have!

Perhaps, like the Samaritan woman, you "know" things about religion and Scripture, but do you really know them to be absolutely true in your heart? This is the goal of our study: To understand that we know both the gift of Him and the gifts from Him.

We need to say goodbye to living vicariously. It's time to realize you and I play the main character we've been talking about in this study. We are the character whose heart would drastically benefit from knowing a pivotal piece of information. It's no longer just a character on a page or screen. This time, you play the female lead.

Yesterday, we mentioned the reason we "pull" for these characters in the movie has to do with the fact we all have a fear of missing out on something.

What are some things you fear missing out on in life?

Do you see a theme of these concerns?

As you take a look at these fears, will you ask the Lord to show you if there is a deeper desire surfacing?

Soak up a key verse from John 4:10, "If you only knew the gift God has for you and who you are speaking to, you would ask me, and I would give you living water" (NLT).

We do not want to miss out on knowing what is available to us through God's promises. If we do, we run the risk of looking back on our lives and saying, "If I had known that—it would have changed . . . well . . . a lot." If we know His presence is always with us, we are also always in the middle of an exciting, surprise encounter with Him. We can look forward to this. He wants to make this real to us.

In 1 John, the apostle makes the point of his letter clear: "I have written these things to you who believe in the name of the Son of God, so that you may know that you have eternal life" (1 John 5:13). Look up the following verses in your Bible and write key phrases of what God wants believers to **know**:

- 1 John 3:16

- 1 John 3:19

- 1 John 3:24

- 1 John 4:16

For many key elements of the Christian life, John, the one who also recorded the true story of the Samaritan woman, wanted to drive home the concept of assurance.

So, what if? What if we were the main character of the "movie" and lived aware of the simultaneous scenes around us, such as: Knowing someone is loyal and will never leave us (Hebrews 13:5)? Knowing an everlasting love (Jeremiah 33:11)? One colleague often uses a similar illustration in marriage counseling: "At the end of the day, you can put up with almost anything just knowing you have someone at home who will listen." With this mindset, we can put up with a lot and anticipate a lot—*just knowing*.

Week 1 Day Four

Yesterday we discussed our desire to not miss out on something God has for us. With that in mind, consider this quote from theologian Francis Schaeffer:

> "I would suggest it is perfectly possible for a
> Christian to be so infiltrated with 20th century thinking that
> he lives most of his life as if the supernatural were not there."[6]

What are your thoughts?

We can identify with pulling for a character in a movie. Hebrews 12:1-2a says, "Therefore, since we also have such a large cloud of witnesses surrounding us, let us lay aside every weight and the sin that so easily ensnares us. Let us run with endurance the race that lies before us, keeping our eyes on Jesus, the source and perfecter of our faith."

How does it make you feel to know you are literally being cheered on as you play out your role in your life movie?

Do you want to know what word sticks out to me? *Run.* This describes the shameless running of a warrior and the carefreeness of a child. Freedom that comes with knowing truth. John 8:32 says, "You will know the truth, and the truth will set you free." This same type of freedom we saw earlier this week from 2 Corinthians 3:17, "Now the Lord is the Spirit, and where the Spirit of the Lord is, there is freedom."

If God met you in the middle of your daily routine, how would He fill in the blanks?

_____ *(write your name),*

"If you only knew . . . really, really knew . . . _____

What is it He's calling you to know right now in your life? What do you think He would tell your heart in light of His Word? Use these answers to fill in the blank above or expound below.

Remember, His goal is for this to be "unveiled reality." He wants His gifts and His truth to be clear and open to you. If you need help answering, try looking up and listing these promises to help spur you forward:

1. Isaiah 62:5b

2. 1 John 1:9

3. Hebrews 13:5-6

4. Romans 10:9

What is God's direct message to you in each of these verses? Finish the sentences below, writing out what God wants you to discover—to know—that you may or may not be living to the full extent:

Isaiah 62:5b **For example:** *"If you only knew . . . that He rejoices when He sees you like a groom seeing His bride."*

(What would you add to this one?)

1 John 1:9
"If you only knew . . . _____

Hebrews 13:5-6
"If you only knew . . . _____

Romans 10:9 "It's the word of faith that welcomes God to go to work and set things right for us. This is the core of our preaching. Say the welcoming word to God—"Jesus is my Master"—embracing, body and soul, God's work of doing in us what he did in raising Jesus from the dead. That's it. You're not "doing" anything; you're simply calling out to God, trusting him to do it for you. That's salvation. With your whole being you embrace God setting things right, and then you say it, right out loud: "God has set everything right between him and me!" (MSG)

"If you only knew . . . _____

Write your favorite conclusion statement from today:

"If I only knew _____ , I would

_____ .*

*This serves as your weekly "Engraving Question" to write on your heart and re-record in the back of this workbook. You can easily look at a snapshot of what the Lord taught you (and to share your experience with others).

Week 1 Day Five

Let's not just pretend you are the main character; let's act on the idea. We've talked about picturing our lives the same way Hollywood sets up the various scenes in a movie. It's important to note that we are not solely focusing on blessings working out behind the scenes. Yes, God could very well be working out a job for you, preparing you a mate—and I rejoice with you if He is! But I'm talking about the kind of daydream we can KNOW. Knowing that He's present when you are lonely. Knowing He is for you when you need a cheerleader. Knowing He is light when darkness surrounds. We are going to use Scripture as our guide to live in unveiled reality regardless of our circumstances. This is very imaginative and different from what we do on a daily basis. Because, as you'll see, if we begin daydreaming differently like this, it will be a game changer. Based on God's Word, let's draw some "split screen" pictures of God's Word and real life. We will begin to taste the peace and joy of merging these two side by side.

The Bible is full of simultaneous scenes, switching back and forth between the Hero, the main character, the friend, and the Enemy. The story of Elijah in 1 Kings 17:5-15 is one great example.

What was Elijah doing (vs. 1-10)?

What was God doing (vs. 8-9)?

What was the woman doing (vs. 10-13)?

To make this application point in our lives, first, let's draw a set of our own scenes from something that has already happened in your life. You might want to draw a picture of when the Lord was faithful to you, even while you had no idea of the result yet. If you have a hard time picturing yourself as an illustrator, feel free to draw simple objects instead of a whole scene, reminding you of a time of His goodness. You can even choose to make words your art. For example, you could use Romans 5:8. In one box, you could write, "While we were still sinners." The next box would read the amazing end of that story, "Christ died for us." If you were the woman of Zarephath, you could write about collecting wood, preparing for the end of life. The next box would contain what God had planned all along during her struggle. We will start with the past scenes because we have lived through the result of these and we can look back and see God's hand. This will spur us on to think in the present tense.

My Perspective	What the Hero was doing in the meantime based on His promises

Sometimes we have to use more faith in the present, but it doesn't make it any less real. A set of scenes from a present situation might look like this: The Lord going before you into a child's bedroom where you need wisdom to handle a sensitive topic (from Deuteronomy 31:8).

Using Scripture, what can you picture God doing in your life in a simultaneous scene though perhaps with physical eyes you see a very different scene in front of you?

My Perspective	What God promises He is doing on my behalf or Who He promises to be

Does a certain Bible verse come to mind when you think of your picture above? If so, jot it down below. If nothing comes to you, don't worry, we will have time in our group setting to go over this. If you are doing this as an individual study, asking a Christian friend to help you would lead to an awesome discussion.

Scripture:

Here's the great part I want to encourage us all with today. You could have so much fun with this.

My dad is known for having unusual reactions to situations. On a recent medical visit, the doctor asked him to point to the stress spots on his body. He paused, cleaned the smudges off his glasses with his shirt and matter-of-factly said, "I don't have any." Seriously. And he wasn't just trying to avoid a more thorough examination. To an almost abnormal point, he truly handles stress better than anyone I've ever known.

He uses this to his advantage in many areas of his life, especially on the basketball court. Don't let the 5'6" stature fool you; it's never stopped him. This guy will pick up a basketball game almost anytime, anywhere, with anyone. If a player is known for being a sore loser, it's almost better to him. Instead of dreading the man's angry reaction, letting him win, or ignoring his offer to play, my father welcomes the challenge. If he wins the game with such a person (which he often does), the opponent does what *he* often does—throws a grown-man fit on the court. All the while, my dad always has a good perspective—"It's just a game." He silently, or sometimes not so silently, laughs at the players who do not share the same mental strategy. A person's true colors have a way of surfacing in competition, and my father enjoys keeping his cool. He knows it is just a game, and he has fun reminding himself of that fact. The laughter is an overflow of the peace he has in the spirit God gave him; although, at times his human side is tempted to laugh out loud at the other player's lack of patience!

All my life, he taught my sister and me the same concept. When we would desire to stand for what is right and face a person in opposition, he listened to our concerns. After hearing us out and addressing how to best handle the problem, he would add his tagline, "You know, you could have so much fun with this!" As you can imagine, with a house full of girls, a variety of situations crossed his radar. He found a way to work this phrase into almost every one of them. And here's what he meant: "If you continue forward with what you know and do what is right, the problem makers will eventually show their true colors. They'll be upset they can't shake you . . . and that will be funny to watch."

So it is with where we are in our lives. This "knowing" we are called to is more than a boring discipline. It's more than the same thing we've heard before. God wants to fill us with the fresh, "living water" knowledge of His promises. When the negative feelings come our way, we can live differently. Consciously living out that which we were previously unaware of is the power we need to laugh at the enemy's attempts, as an overflow of our knowledge of God's truth.

You can live the life of knowing who you are and Whose you are. Bypass the enemy. Have the answer to your heart's desire. Open up your ears to the Good News. He's saying it right now, "I, the one speaking to you—I am he."

The One who can give us a gift to silence our loneliness, disappointment, and fears . . . is closer than you think.

You could have so much fun with this.

Nightlight:

Write John 4:10 in the space below:

Defensive Strategies for a Well-Accessorized Mind

Week 2 Day One

The choice seems obvious. Of course, we'll take the life-changing news. Of course, the woman wanted the never-ending water. Why, then, do we struggle to live like we have been offered such a gift?

Another common element in a movie plot is interference. Something is keeping the main character from knowing the news the audience wants her to discover. From the spectator's vantage point, we so urgently want the person causing the interference to be found out in his schemes.

The 2001 romantic comedy *Serendipity* presents a dynamic example of this. Actress Kate Beckinsale plays Sara Thomas, a believer in "fate." She hastily runs into a Waldorf Hotel elevator and tells her date, Jonathan (played by John Cusack), to jump on a separate elevator. She sets up the challenge: if they both choose the same floor to stop on, they were meant to be together. The man thinks this is ridiculous because—what are the chances of their choosing the same floor? But seeing as he does not have a better option than to leave his new crush all together, he goes along with it. She chooses floor 23; he chooses floor 23. It seems golden at this point.

But prior to reaching the 23rd floor, Jonathan's elevator stops to let on a father and son duo. As if that were not enough to ruin the timing, the mischievous son proceeds to hit every button on the number pad, sabotaging the route.

Meanwhile, Sara sits on the carpet landing, waiting on her chosen, 23rd floor. Jonathan simultaneously picks up more and more people on his elevator until he has convinced the passengers with his story to stop at each floor, searching for his lost, almost nameless, maiden. Sara gives up after sometime and seamlessly steps onto a descending elevator just as Jonathan finally arrives with his posse to a vacant 23rd floor. End of scene.

The costume choice for the character of the little boy on the elevator was no "fortunate accident." The boy, dressed in a shiny, red devil costume, becomes an unmistakable visual to show us the role Satan attempts to play in our lives. His motive is to interfere with us really knowing God's gift.

Read 1 Peter 5:8. What is the warning we see here?

What feeling does this stir in you as you picture Satan acting as this enemy attempting to derail you from your desired destination?

Does this make you angry in a righteous way? _____

Let's not shy away from the anger and aggravation we feel in the movie towards the child's action that prevents the two people from meeting. We should welcome righteous anger against the Enemy in this situation as he *attempts* to rule and interrupt our lives.

Therefore, awareness is not just for us to know the gift of God. We must also be aware of the efforts of the Enemy so we can safeguard our mind and heart. After all, he may be pushing the buttons, but we are responsible for whether or not we get off at each floor.

Tomorrow we will begin to examine, in detail, a few "elevator buttons," or ways Satan tries to slow us down. For now, let's continue with this notion that something must be done about this. In the midst of this interference and all-out war for our mindfulness, what do we have going for us?

Ephesians 6:10 says, "Finally, be strengthened by the Lord and by his *vast strength*" [emphasis mine].

Continue on to verse 11. What does it tell us we have access to?

Isn't that amazing?

Read Ephesians 6:16. What do we learn here?

When are we supposed to put this on?

How many attacks is it good for?

Last year my son, Hunter, drew a watercolor picture with the acronym TFSJ. He was all of six years old . . . so you can imagine my perplexity in guessing the picture with such a caption. I mean, this could be anything, right? He told me matter-of-factly the letters stood for "The Favorite Shield, Jesus." Let your heart ponder that. God has given Hunter the same shield He's offering to us—The Favorite Shield, Jesus. Furthermore in Ephesians 6, we read specifically that the shield of faith is to extinguish all the flaming arrows of the evil one. And we aren't talking about a small, frying-pan size, either. Shields in this particular biblical time were large enough for a whole body to crouch behind. Let's get the imagery around this. When we believe so solidly in Jesus, our shield, our best protection—we do not merely deflect, we EXTINGUISH all the flaming arrows of the Evil One.

Will you take up the shield of faith today?

Write a prayer to The Favorite Shield, Jesus. The One and Only.

Week 2 Day Two

Today we will look at three attempts of enemy interference that can hinder us from fully knowing the gift of our God. We'll explore a little on each one and decide where we need to strategize (pray) against being the Enemy's prey.

1. DISTRACTION

Have you ever heard the phrase "If Satan can't make you 'bad,' he'll make you busy"? What do you think is meant by that?

Satan wants to distract us so that we buy into the fact that we just don't have time to think about God—that thoughts of Him never enter our minds in the first place.

How do the following verses spur you on to minimize distraction so that we may contemplate our Lord? Write your answers below each verse.

Psalm 46:10a "Be still and know that I am God" (NIV).

Psalm 131:1-2 "My heart is not proud, Lord, my eyes are not haughty; I do not concern myself with great matters or things too wonderful for me. But I have calmed and quieted myself, I am like a weaned child with its mother; like a weaned child I am content" (NIV).

Luke 10:39 "She had a sister called Mary, who sat at the Lord's feet listening to what he said" (NIV).

Deuteronomy 6:4-9 "Hear, O Israel: The Lord our God, the Lord is one. Love the Lord your God with all your heart and with all your soul and with all your strength. These commandments that I give you today are to be on your hearts. Impress them on your children. Talk about them when you sit at home and when you walk along the road, when you lie down and when you get up. Tie them as symbols on your hands and bind them on your foreheads. Write them on the doorframes of your houses and on your gates" (NIV).

Psalm 62:5a "Let all that I am wait quietly before God" (NLT).

Psalm 130:5-6 "I wait for Yahweh; I wait and put my hope in His word. I wait for the Lord more than watchmen wait for the morning—more than watchmen for the morning."

2. UNBELIEF

I'm either the most qualified or most under qualified to write this. I'm going to humbly go with most qualified because God's grace is sufficient in my weakness. My seasons of doubt have never made God less God. And the fact that God is not pleased with disbelief, but still gently loves and corrects, leaves me with the conclusion that His strength is perfected in my weakness. He is the most worthy of my faith.

2 Corinthians 12:8-10 refers to God's grace as an abundance for our weakness. Read these verses. Have you experienced a time when your faith was weak but His grace was greater in spite of it? If not, can you allow yourself to believe that it is?

Also, let's be encouraged by one of my favorite verses—Psalm 94:19 "When doubts fill my mind, your comfort gave me renewed hope and cheer" (NLT). Praise Him.

Mark 9 tells the story of a father who comes to Jesus for the healing of his son. Jesus tells him that everything is possible for the man who has faith. In response to this, the man cries out, "I do believe! Help my unbelief" (v. 24).

There are times, yes, when we wrestle with our faith. At the end of this trial or wrestling should be a victorious assurance of faith, a strengthening. It can be a process, and it is not always a quick fix for sure, but there needs to be faith in the One.

What does Hebrews 11:6 tell us about God's desire?

The *Holman Christian Standard Bible* says the last part of the verse this way: ". . . the one who draws near to Him must believe that He exists and rewards those who seek Him." He is going to accept our coming to Him with arms open wide, and it's a must that we believe that.

Read Deuteronomy 1:29-34. Does God take our faith in Him seriously?

How did He feel when the Israelites refused to believe?

This verse calls me to action almost every time I read it. The action is usually a prayer to not be like the Israelites described in verse 32.

We also know the flipside is true based on what we just read in Hebrews 11:6. How pleased is He when we believe! Remember, the One who calls us to believe is the same One who has unlimited mercy on us and who helps us grow in our faith. In this verse, the Israelites received the consequences of their lack of faith. If unbelief reigns in our lives, we will also miss out on many promised lands God intends for us.

The Bible makes it very clear. In many miracles, the Lord said the person's faith in Him healed him or her. If you are struggling to believe, tell Him. And then through the Spirit and His Word, err on the side of faith. *Way on the side of faith.*

As a little kid, I remember sitting on my grandpa's lap having theological discussions with him. He would pose the question, "Can God make a rock so big that He could not pick it up?" The question presents an understanding that there's nothing God cannot do. The Scripture says nothing is impossible with God. (Matthew 19:26). Except . . . 2 Timothy 2:13 tells us there actually is something He cannot do. He cannot go against His character. He is faithful, even when we are faithless. This should call us even more to put our faith in Him. But Satan tries to get us to rely on ourselves and question God's Word. The words "but Satan" have not an ounce of power when the Gospel always screams "but God . . ."

Leave your book open where you'll be sure to see it tonight so you can remember to answer the Nightlight below.

Nightlight:

Which Scripture reference that we studied today means the most to you in your life right now, and why?

Week 2 Day Three

Today we continue to identify more obstacles that need to be grasped. As we read over these, I pray *against* condemnation and *for* healing and a quicker route to knowing God's gift.

The first two methods we uncovered were:
1. Distraction
2. Unbelief

Let's look at the next three:

3. BEING EASILY IMPRESSED

On one hand, this could be considered distraction as well. On the other hand, this could be deliberate sin—having an idol. It's what we do every time we dwell on the neat things of this world at the expense of knowing Jesus.

Consider these verses:

1 Samuel 2:2 "There is no one holy like the LORD. There is no one besides You! And there is no rock like our God."

Psalm 84:10-11 "Better a day in Your courts than a thousand anywhere else. I would rather be at the door of the house of my God than to live in the tents of wicked people. For the LORD God is a sun and shield. The LORD gives grace and glory; He does not withhold the good from those who live with integrity."

Read John 4:11 and John 4:15 in our text about the Samaritan woman. Was she willing to forsake what she KNEW, the familiarity of the known, for what was promised from the Lord? How can you tell?

She pulled out one of the highest names she could think of and referenced Jacob, from the Patriarch Hall of Fame. Little did the woman at the well know she was talking to Jacob's Maker. How many times do we miss God's presence in our day because of satisfaction with lesser things?

What are some of the lesser things you are tempted to rely on or be attracted to more than our God?

4. IMPURITY AND UNREPENTANT SIN

God calls us to holiness, not harmony, with the same lens as the rest of the world. We need to know this button is dangerous and a major player in keeping us from knowing the gift of God. Let us seriously ask the Lord if there is anything offensive in us and for Him to point it out (see Psalm 139:24). Then we can see more clearly. "Blessed are the pure in heart, for they will see God" (Matthew 5:8, NIV).

How determined are you to be set apart for the Lord?

1   2   3   4   5   6   7   8   9   10

unmotivated   *absolutely*

He also knows the consequences of sin, including the physical, emotional, and spiritual consequences. Not to mention the spiritual dirtiness we put on ourselves when we sin. The distractions of impurities in this world rob our hearts from the good stuff. Psalm 101:3a states, "I will not set anything worthless before my eyes." This covenant of David paints a picture of a face firmly set, unshaken and determined not to go there.

God calls us to be holy. "But just as he who called you is holy, so be holy in all you do; for it is written: "**Be holy, because I am holy**" (1 Peter 1:15-16 NIV). Most people rub this off as impossible, stiff, and religious. But God recently showed me something so lovely about this. His holiness is as white as the thickest snow. It's absolutely clean. And the best part is that God wants us to be like Him. God is called "Holy, Holy, Holy." He is called this as His repetitive attribute in Scripture. Now think of someone who annoys you. I'm just being honest here; I sure don't welcome a person like that to take on who I am. The flesh side of us is quite content and often prefers distance. I do not necessarily find it natural to desire for another person to be just like me. But that is exactly what God wants. Us. Sinners. Wayward children. He wants us to be like Him.

Let that sink in. Stop the study right here if you need to meditate on this.

5. BEING JADED AND CYNICAL

We'll start off discussing this button by listing some biblical songs (Hunter calls these "God Songs") you currently sing to your children, nieces, nephews, or children at church. (If you haven't been around children lately, what would some go-to songs be if given the chance?)

Choose one song and write the lyrics as you can remember. Feel free to look online if you need additional help.

Now underline the lyrics you would keep if you were to look in the face of a child and tell him "this is absolutely true."

Next, highlight the lyrics you believe are true for you. Be honest here. Which ones do you truly believe in your heart?

What does this reveal to you about what we believe for ourselves versus what we believe for our children?

Let's do our exercise again from last week. How would you fill in the blanks with this idea of the song lyrics and what you've just journaled?

If I only knew _____,

I would _____

_____ .

Let this not be true of us, women of God! We sing songs to children like "God Is So Good" and "He's Got the Whole World in His Hands," but we live like it's only true until you reach a certain age! Forgive us, Lord. Ironically, we really want our children to believe these promises. Deep down, we know they contain life, yet we default to feeling like our day-to-day zaps the life right out of us. It's great to believe these things for our children, but we have to believe it fully, which includes believing the promises are for us as adults to claim as well. Pray and ask God to open your heart to child-like faith again. When I find myself thinking, "Oh, how cute for the little ones," I gently remind myself those lyrics and stories were meant for us as "big kids," too.

Look up Matthew 18:3 and Romans 8:15 and record your thoughts.

Be encouraged, my dear friend. Like we discussed in the topic of unbelief, even when we have trouble believing for ourselves, God helps us with this. God is the One to take us by the hand, look us in the eye and say "This is absolutely true for you."

End your study time writing a prayer below to the Lord—praying for His help against one of these interferences. I'd encourage you to go ahead and thank Him for His help . . . He lives for it, actually (Hebrews 7:25).

Tomorrow we'll address the sixth and final obstacle to avoid.

Week 2 Day Four

The final interference tactic used by Satan can be viewed as a summary of the previous five. The biggie. The final fireworks of the show. If Satan were pushing a button on your elevator to slow you down, this one would be the red master button linked to all the others. You get the idea.

We can be drawn to things that glisten or look like a fireworks display. Fish are lured by something that looks good to them, but ends in death, and *so it is with us* (on this one). Now let's be clear: to take away our attraction to shiny objects would be to rip out part of the DNA of a woman. I would never make such a suggestion. This is about mental habits formed from false thoughts. The ones that loop over and over in your head with such repetition they begin to take on the appearance of truth. Maybe they didn't start off shiny and attractive, but over time we give them trophy position in our minds without even knowing it.

I'm talking about the interference of *Repeated, False Thoughts*.

From the title of this alone, can you see how this button of lies becomes ammo for the previous five danger zones? Please note we are focusing on how it is linked to all the others. It is not more powerful than unrepentant sin.

Just for a second, go back to our list:

1. Distraction
2. Unbelief
3. Being Easily Impressed
4. Impurity and Unrepentant Sin
5. Being Jaded and Cynical

Which one did you feel God wanted you to focus on extinguishing? Which one did the Holy Spirit reveal as one that is "in the way" of your fully knowing the gift of God? Flip through your notes in the previous pages if you need to refresh your memory (I honestly had to for myself when I got to this point!)

With this in mind, what might be a repeated, false thought that Satan puts in your mind with regard to this distraction?

Engraving Question:

What Scripture verse will you hide in your heart to combat this so that it no longer has a place in your life? (with the help of the Holy Spirit, of course).

On the flip side, is there an interference you've been able to overcome? Maybe God is whispering a victory lap to you about this . . . "We've moved past this one."

This is something to celebrate!

If so, what false idea associated with it have you dispelled from your life?

I love my hometown, but it's a well-known fact that in Houston, we barely get a fall season. Summer especially wore out its welcome a few years ago with record highs well past August. In the few crisp days that ushered in some breezy hope for us, everyone went crazy. I've always found it interesting how one can actually smell a chill in the autumn air. I think my husband thought I was crazy, but on the first few cool days, I excitedly announced to him that I could almost smell the plastic, tingling strands of stars and cowbells welcoming homecoming season.

That same fall season a new theme came to our city: The vacant buildings did a disappearing act. Houston is not known to have vacant buildings, and in fact, I did not know most of them were vacant until they were labeled otherwise. Let me explain. The Barnes and Noble in a premier corner lot of the Galleria, the PetSmart, and the two-story Academy on the interstate—just to name a few—all had one thing in common. New fluorescent orange banners were draped over the former tattered signage. In every building, the vacancy light was turned off quickly and Halloween retail filled the "empty" spaces.

I like a good fall festival with the church; I enjoy the kiddos in costumes and neighborhood candy raids. But darkness, scariness, and anything that celebrates death more than life, I can't cherish. Because of the background of the "holiday," we know some people use Halloween as a day laced with evil motives. This knowledge, along with how quickly the stores set up shop, is what struck me about the vacant buildings. One was even labeled "The Spirit of Halloween." The signage was obviously temporary, and yet, as they remained throughout the fall, we almost got used to them being there.

Likewise, we have to be sure that as we are changing our minds and eliminating negative thinking patterns, we are replacing them with something. Our minds do not have the capability to sit empty. If we are not careful to replace our thoughts with truth from the Lord, something is sure to take up residence. Lot value in Houston is pricy; imagine the dollar amount the Enemy puts on the square footage of our minds. It's too valuable for vacancy.

What does Romans 8:37 and 1 John 4:4 say about who we are?

According to these verses, why are we that?

No vacancy here.

In the next three days we'll specifically address the impact of the sixth button and how to overcome it. Now that we know what to watch out for, we'll discuss the importance of preparing an offensive weapon to know God's gift. Make no mistake; our God is One who completes. He won't tell us what *not* to do without complementing that with something *to* do. Perhaps the biggest revelation will come when we realize this victory is actually attainable.

What does that mean for you to know that God is a Completer?

Aren't you glad God isn't just into "cleaning house" and leaving an empty space? He wants us to be "fully pleasing to Him, bearing fruit in every good work and growing in the knowledge of God" (Colossians 1:10b).

How are we described at the very beginning of this verse?

What causes this life, and what is the result (vs. 9-10)?

Not just the absence of bad fruit . . . a full harvest of that which is sweet and good.

"Therefore, brothers, by the mercies of God, I urge you to present your bodies as a living sacrifice, holy and pleasing to God; this is your spiritual worship. Do not be conformed to this age, but be transformed by the renewing of your mind, so that you may discern what is the good, pleasing and perfect will of God."

Romans 12:1-2

It's my sincere prayer we learn this together.

Nightlight:

Re-read the verse you listed for your Engraving Question for "combat" today. Or, if you couldn't think of one earlier, return to it now.

et's face it, "unhappily accessorized" sounds much more couture than "emotional baggage." The point is—because of those repeated, false thoughts—we're still unhappier than necessary. And the sooner we realize our minds are unhappily accessorized, we're one step closer to exchanging our feelings for those vibrant ones we all desire.

Each emotion we have can be traced back to a thought. Suppose you were to look at a map. All emotions you experience—positive, negative, and neutral—are represented as cities. Imagine you pointed to a certain emotion and wanted to backtrack to see how you got there. The connecting highways, bridges, and streets are our thoughts. One particular city, or emotion, might look like a big spider web, with many "roads" leading to its entrance. Another feeling might have one long connecting road representing one thought leading to another connecting thought leading to another thought and finally to a strong emotion. At any rate, the good news is the feelings are retraceable, which means they are workable, and there's something we can do about them.

Thoughts lead to feelings . . . do you believe this to be true for you? Why or why not? Give an example of when you know your thoughts influenced your feelings.

While I thoroughly enjoy artsy home projects, I would not say I am an innately crafty person. Maybe I have some creative ideas, but a craft gene? No. I literally walked around my friend's kitchen with a pen and clipboard while she so effortlessly gave verbal instructions on how to decorate sugar cookies with royal icing. I had to write it down. Every.

Single. Step. I truly admire friends who can take a couple of classes and can (with honesty) add "sewing" and "cake decorating" to their list of Facebook hobbies. This girl here just needs a little more direction to even make the attempt. So, just in case you are similar in the learning department, the following pages provide concrete details in this process of mental re-accessorizing.

Therapist Albert Ellis, a forerunner for this principle of how our thoughts affect our feelings, developed what we know and still use today as REBT (Rational Emotive Behavioral Therapy) and the technique of RSA (Rational Self-Analysis).

The basic concept of RSA can be broken down into the identification of four things:

1. The emotion
2. The situation surrounding the emotion
3. Specific thoughts linked to the emotion
4. What to use in place of those thoughts

Example of how to fill in the first three steps:

1. Emotion: Anxiety
2. Situation: Awaiting test results at a doctor's office
3. Specific thoughts: What if it is untreatable? What if I have to miss more work? My boss won't understand. I'll be unable to take care of my family. My kids will have needs only I can fill. My life is a rollercoaster. My life is over.

What does this mean for us? The ideas in this theory give us a launching pad for practical application as we uncover the Enemy's whispers and reveal the under-claimed gifts of God.

While the first two blanks, labeling the emotion and the situation, are pretty easy, we need to go one layer deeper and list our thoughts. It's normal to say, "I'm angry, tired, or upset." It's normal to say this to a friend and then explain the situation. But the thought territory is often unchartered, and we tend not to go there. The thoughts surrounding our feelings become part of us. In the last week, we discussed the danger of false thoughts being left alone. They start off as lies, and over time, without rebuttal, they make a pseudo-home in us. They become the false "treasures" of our minds.

Read 2 Corinthians 10:4-5:

"The weapons of our warfare are not worldly, but are powerful through God for the demolition of strongholds. We demolish arguments and every high-minded thing that is raised up against the knowledge of God, taking every thought captive to obey Christ."

What does this say about our weapons?

What are they used for?

How does this relate to our verses from Ephesians we read in Day One of this week?

"Finally, be strengthened by the Lord and by His vast strength. Put on the full armor of God so that you can stand against the tactics of the Devil" (Ephesians 6:10-11).

The Expositor's Bible Commentary states that "every thought" mentioned in 2 Corinthians 10:5 "means every human device that temporarily frustrates the divine plan."[7]

What conclusions can you make with this definition?

I'll share a few of mine. If it's temporary, this gives me reassurance that victory is inevitable for those of us in Christ. It also makes me think that it's human thinking that thwarts; therefore, my own thinking needs to be changed. Sometimes the source may be words spoken over me that I have adopted as truth; sometimes, it is all my own thinking. Nevertheless, Satan uses our wrong thoughts to frustrate God's desire for our lives.

We'll have no need to "re-accessorize" our minds unless a problem has been identified. Any thought repeated often enough has the potential of falling into the truth bucket of our minds. The beliefs become all the subtler as the repetition continues. They also become vaguer. Once we realize what thoughts are surrounding a certain emotion, we can sift through and determine which ones are false. We'll see there is much value in the process of slowing down to search, clarify, and ultimately remove them as reality. I like to call this "Off the Hook" therapy. This gives us complete license, with the Lord's leading, to "unbelieve" some of the thoughts that have haunted us for the majority of life. It's like a new prognosis. Our lives don't have to play the same background music over and over again in our heads. We're off the hook. It's each woman's responsibility to change her thoughts. She no longer has to shoulder the burden they provide.

Look up Proverbs 13:19 and write it below.

May we not get so stuck on the work it takes to change that we forfeit the dream, the desire—the sweet taste of God that He has for us.

Specific Gifts You Can Know

gain, this whole idea of changing our thoughts can sound good on paper, but when it comes to what it looks like in real life, it can seem a little fuzzy. Let's try out what we've learned with our friend, the Samaritan woman. Refresh yourself with the story from John 4:1-25 for clues on how she was likely thinking and feeling.

We'll take some of the main emotions she was likely experiencing and take her through these steps, linking her feelings back to a thought source.

You'll notice as we lay the foundation of the first three steps (pinpointing the emotion, situation and specific thoughts), the new, replacement thoughts are put on hold. Before we get into the detailed replacement thoughts, we will practice the first few steps. Then we'll add on the sweetest part of the deal.

Coaching the Woman at the Well

1. EMOTION: FEARFUL/ANXIOUS

Situation: *Afraid of being seen or confronted in public, afraid of being left again*

Possible Thought Chain: Let's get this over with. I hate going out in public—all those sneers and comments. They think I can't hear them. I'm going to walk fast—with my head down. Goodness, I hope they can't see my heart pounding through my clothes. What if I go to all this trouble, and I still have to face them? Maybe that's giving them too much credit. I've got to take charge—control my situation. Maybe then I'll have the minimal amount of ridicule. Just like I have to control the situation at home—you know—be on top of things. I have to anticipate what my man will say, even if it means I am walking on eggshells all my waking hours. I can't do or say anything that would make him leave me again. What if he does? That's my worst fear. So I live in fear and do everything I can to prevent it. I've learned if I expect the worst, it seems to soften the blow when reality comes.

And it always eventually comes, right? I told myself I would not think about his leaving this time, but the thought absolutely consumes me. I'm rethinking the events of last night. Did I do anything to upset him? He didn't say he loved me. I wonder why. I'm wondering in my head, but I feel the fear in my stomach. What if I mess this up? What if I have to live the rest of my life like this? I think I feel sick.

Specific Thought Summary:
- I can control the situation.
- If I do everything "right," he will love me.
- I can prevent him from being angry and leaving.
- It's my fault if I'm rejected.

Replacement Thoughts: To be continued

Now you have the chance to try it. Where there are blanks already filled out as prompts, add other emotions or situations leading to the emotion. Go for it! Ask the Holy Spirit for help and insight. Don't worry about the replacement thoughts yet. We will get to that soon.

2. EMOTION: ISOLATED, LONELY, LEFT OUT

Situation: *Purposely walking to the well alone, lack of connection with the man who lives with her*

Possible Thought Chain: (What thoughts do you imagine were looping through her head?)

Specific Thought Summary: (in other words, "What is the real message?")
- I must keep this all inside and hide how I really feel.
- The closest I will ever get to companionship is continuing to chase men.

- Your note/thoughts
- Your note/thoughts
- Your note/thoughts

Replacement Thoughts: To be continued

3. EMOTION: UNLOVED, UNWANTED, INVISIBLE

Situation: *The woman's failed relationships in the past*

Possible Thought Chain: Each time I start a new relationship, I hope with all my heart the person will love me. I could list off name after name of those who haven't. The problem must be me. I'm tired of trying. This feeling is unfortunately familiar. Here comes that voice again . . .

Would you add anything else here?

Specific Thought Summary:

- I am a drain on people; I identify myself in this way.
- Your note/thoughts

- Your note/thoughts

Replacement Thoughts: To be continued

Maybe as you read about the woman's feelings, you can think of some of your own. For now, if you can see how the Samaritan woman's thoughts led to certain feelings (some very valid, no doubt), take this time to jot down a few of your own emotions, a situation, and maybe start taking notes on a thought chain. This doesn't have to be neat or formal. Ask the Lord to help you get started. Consider this like our Post-it® note work section. Give your mind a chance to leave some things here to work on later.

Now we have seen, hypothetically, the Samaritan woman's feelings, her thoughts behind the feelings, and the direct beliefs she might have held as a result of the mental habits. How could we challenge these thoughts? Perhaps we could point out she was exerting a false sense of control. She was acting on a lot of "what ifs" instead of absolute facts, and it was making her sick. She was trying to live in perfection as if she was not human. We could also pick a few thoughts here and there and encourage the woman not to "awfulize" the situation.

These pointers could be helpful; however, like many of our lives, when you get to the replacement part, her situation is complicated. After all, for the woman at the well, her thoughts appear to be true. Honestly, wouldn't it be tiring to try and convince the Samaritan woman she was loved or had no need to fear abandonment? The facts are there, and it all adds up. She feels guilty; she has a live-in lover. She feels lonely; she has no friends. She feels she may be left again; she's been through five marriages. So, where do we go from here? The circumstances might lead us to hopelessness in this endeavor. And boy, does the Enemy want us to see it this way. Thoughts based on circumstance provide no security, as events in our lives are constantly changing. However, I cannot blame the woman for basing her thoughts on her circumstances. At this point, it is all she had.

Only because she had yet to meet Jesus.

Only that.

In her encounter with Jesus, we learn two umbrella truths, which can answer many of the weighty emotions we face as women. We'll go over these in detail in Days 3, 4 and 5 of this week. Friends, if you and I can accept these two ideas—really, really believe them to be true for us— there's no cap to our joy. Remember in Week 2, we encouraged each other to err way on the side of belief!

Spend some time in prayer today thinking of all you were pre-Jesus. As you symbolically put your finger on that place in your history, thank God, and praise His name for all the changes in your life since that defining point.

THE BROKEN ECHO

The words of the Enemy repeat in my head,
Why do I nod my heart as if to believe?
When I hear a skewed description of You, or an accusation of me?

It's my acceptance of the same old words,
Steals my joy and keeps me hurt.

I come to the water well both expectant and unsure
Feeling broken and uneasy
But I know you are the cure.

Into the canyon of the well, I pour in exactly what I hear,
"I'm a coward!!!"
Your response takes me by surprise,
"I love you!" comes back even louder.

He says, "I see it all, and I want you to know,
The only thing broken now . . .

Is the echo."

See Isaiah 54:17

Week 3 Day Two

Today, I want to you to know that we are talking about hope that will *last*.

Read 1 Peter 1:23-25.

*Our birth into God's family is*_____ *not*

_____ .

How does the Scripture contrast creation from the Word of the Creator?

There is a reason this section is not titled "10 Steps to Happy Thoughts." Our culture enjoys positive thinking. It gives a sense of control and promises a better life. But positive thinking has its limits and therefore, it is not the final answer for the joy we seek.

I respect the approach taken by Backus and Chapian in their book, *Telling Yourself the Truth*. The authors present the solution as just that: dispute the false beliefs by habitually telling yourself the truth about various emotions including anger, anxiety, and depression.[8] The phrase, "Tell yourself the truth" has more weight than saying, "Think positive thoughts." Think about the limitations of the latter piece of advice.

Positive can help for a little while. You can coast on positive. There comes a time when the coasting is over, and you're out of gas. Strictly positive thinking is too shallow to be beneficial. Sometimes there's no truth to back up happy thoughts. The feel-good statement provides more damage than even temporary relief.

There's a billboard I pass almost every day. Juxtaposed to the plain matte billboards, no matter how many times I pass it, the special LED lights practically lunge at my eyes.

The bright beams advertise the sensitive business of a fertility clinic. Since the billboard is made of special lighting, every once in a while, the slogans rotate. One day the cluster of lights particularly caught my attention as I had never seen this particular advertisement. Three words, one huge promise: "You Can Conceive." I was speechless. How could they say that? My heart pounds as I think of women who long to have children. The billboard wording is probably encouraging to some and maddening for others further along the infertility course with no change of their maternity status. What is accomplished if a woman tells herself this phrase over and over again? I have a friend who literally does not have a womb. How would she feel if she saw that billboard? The marketer probably had good intentions. God has used fertility clinics in the lives of many families, and the clinic was trying to offer a solution through their billboard. I get it. But feel the massive weight of possible emptiness in those three words. They simply are not true for every driver who passes those lights.

Have you ever experienced this before? Have you ever read or heard of something that sounded good, but it turned out to be a promise lacking substance?

I'd like to introduce you to my friend, Jessica. She's a fabulous thirty-eight-year-old woman who waited and tried and waited again to be a mommy. She attended the baby showers, held and celebrated all of our babies—all the while in a season of "not yet" for her own. Jessica is a gorgeous blonde with lagoon, blue-green eyes, and yet, the time came when those eyes landscaped with hope and promise were replaced with sorrow and isolation. Humanly speaking, you can only hear the words, "I'm sorry" and "It will happen in God's timing" so many times. She and her husband tried oral medication, seven rounds of IUI and four transfers of IVF. They grieved heavily as they lost one baby boy at 22 weeks through IUI and four other babies through IVF. These were babies with known genders. They were named. People tried to comfort Jessica, but even their encouragement was empty. She knew people meant well, but unlike the billboard in the sky, there was no guarantee she would become a mother. So positive thinking did nothing to lift her spirits.

Jessica readily traces the feelings of isolation and stolen joy back to these lies from the Enemy. They quickly came to mind, as he had repeated them to her frequently:

- I can't talk to adults—I don't know what to say.
- I will just disappoint people who say they have been praying for me for so long.
- Obviously, I wouldn't be a good mom.
- God is pushing me away.

Amidst these raw emotions of saying goodbye to baby after baby, Jessica shared something quite bizarre. She said with every loss, "It got easier for me every time."

Huh?

She meant what she said.

Jessica decided to make a conscious effort to do something about these irrational thoughts. It surely didn't happen in one day, but conscious effort over time led her to fully embrace *these* beliefs instead:

- This is not what God is trying to do; He's not trying to push me away.
- I need to engage in God's Word and in others.
- I can use the blessings He has already given to me.

Friends, these are absolutely her exact words.

Specifically, the major verses Jessica and her husband purposefully told themselves over and over were Psalm 16:11 and Philippians 1:3-6. Psalm 16:11 says, "You will make known to me the path of life; In your presence is fullness of joy; In your right hand there are pleasures forever" (NASB). The truth for her in this verse was that God is always right there—for her—and His face is always joyful. She had to choose to believe that. And if His face was always joyful, then there was something to be joyful about. She said, "I could either look to Him or look to the wall [in isolation]." They claimed this truth from the Philippians verse: "God has a plan for us and He *will* work on it until Christ returns."

And so, with each baby lost, there was absolutely proper grief and disappointment, but it became easier because Jessica was literally clutching these truths that came truer with time and faith.

These are the truths that are more than positive thinking for Jessica. The ones she said do not turn up empty:

- He will answer prayer in some way, even if it's not the way we wanted.

- He does not leave your heart's desires void.
- I have to trust God in my motherhood.
- He's not going to leave you void.
- He is faithful regardless.
- He's still my God.

This model of claiming truth is more than positive thinking because, in a nutshell, it has to be. Positive thinking comes so easy to our world today. *Just tell yourself what you want to hear.* But we can believe beyond that. Not only to set ourselves apart (even though it is reason enough), but because our souls need more.

Recall from Week One: Day Four in John 8:31-32, Jesus says, "If you continue in My word, you really are My disciples. You will know the truth, and the truth will set you free." This is the freedom that makes one free, like a key that turns the door. Jesus said if you hold on to my teachings, then you will be free, a literal ushering out from the hold of sin.

What do you see in Isaiah 55:6-12?

What things do we learn are "higher" in verse 9?

Telling yourself God's truth is so much better than anything else. Read Ephesians 3:20-21.

I love what Kelly Matte, our pastor's wife, said in a women's Bible study about Ephesians 3:20. Often we think the verse says God can do more of what we ask or imagine. But that's not it. It's not more of the same. The verse says He is "able to do *above and beyond* all that we ask or think" [emphasis mine]. It's a completely different and BETTER plan or dream for us. Praise Him!

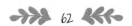

It gets even better.

Rank the following in order of what is best (4th place, 3rd place, 2nd place, 1st place):

Reminding myself of the truth

God's truth spoken over me

Habitual, false thinking

Positive thinking

Although first and second place are light years beyond the others, a step above telling ourselves the truth is hearing God's truth spoken over us. I believe in what C.S. Lewis states when he says, "All truth is God's truth." It's the same truth; let's just rejoice in where it originates. Sometimes we just need to take a deep breath and tell ourselves, "Everything is going to be ok." There's nothing wrong with that. But, what difference does it make to have someone Who loves you and Who is protective over you, Who knows the future and would never lie, remind you, "It's going to be ok"? Feel the difference? All truth is God's truth. Jesus told the woman at the well, "If you only knew the gift God has for you and who you are speaking to . . ." Ah, what refreshment to hear it from this source!

Do you agree? Is there a difference in who sends you the message? Could you give an example of two different people telling you the same thing, but it would mean more coming from one over the other?

What false thought and what truth from Jessica's story can you apply to a situation in your life today?

Can you attach this truth to any notes you might have jotted down in yesterday's lesson (from page 57)?

Now that we know we are dealing with more hope than positive thinking, we'll return to the specifics we need to add as we "coach the woman at the well." The rest of our week will be devoted to the tangible truths we can offer to her as hope. I. Can't. Wait.

Week 3 — Day Three

One day while I was folding laundry, checking emails, and unloading the dishwasher all at the same time, I flipped on the TV just as the cameras shot to a young woman on the couch of *The Today Show*. She was cute, modestly dressed, and her unfamiliar, almost humble wave at the camera made me want to stick through the commercials to hear what gave her a slot on the infamous interview couch. After the break, the talk show hosts began discussing the guest's book. Key words told me it was a story of redemption—coming back home from a past of drugs, stripping, and a major role at The Playboy Mansion. This collegiate-looking blonde named Kendra Wilkinson was coming off the heels of a life with Hefner.

Even in the brevity of a morning show interview, much was revealed. One interviewer commented about the young woman's feelings for Hefner, and without even batting an eye, she clearly affirmed, "I've always loved him." The ex-mansion resident went on to describe how Hefner was "kind" to her. The host brought up something else about Kendra's past which she confirmed—her father abandoned the family when she was a little girl.

In her book, she writes about when Hefner asked her to be his girlfriend:

> "Staring into his eyes, I didn't see a man four times my age with ten
> times more girlfriends than most. Even though I hardly knew him yet,
> I saw a sweet man who made me feel really good about myself—a
> true gentleman. It was weird but in my heart, I felt like
> he was someone I could possibly trust."[9]

The truth is, promiscuity does not always find its origin in fathers without integrity. Likewise, because God can step in and provide a miracle—fathers without character or presence do not guarantee relationship disaster. God can intervene in the life of a woman who has had a poor relationship with her father and rescue a heart from experiencing further scars. It happens, and a healthy, Christian marriage can follow.

While promiscuity is not always derived from a father's character, there is a strong relationship between the two. If a father has been emotionally unavailable, as the daughter goes out into the world, there is a hole in her heart she naturally wants to fill with something. In the book, *Father Hunger*, Dr. Robert S. McGee writes, "Due to misconceptions and faulty definitions, the promise of trust and intimacy combined sounds too attractive for many young adults to refuse. Rejected as children, we grew up feeling a desperation for closeness."[10]

What are specific things you seek from a father figure?

Is this similar to your main desires from other male relationships as well? How?

Here are three I believe rank at the top for women as we seek love from both a father figure and from male relationships in general:

1. Companionship
2. Protection
3. Exclusive Adoration

My son Hunter wants to be a writer when he grows up, so naturally he's been interested in the process of this Bible study. Although I completed the content for this section quite some time ago, I recently asked him what he would write if I gave him three blanks to describe a Daddy's job. Without hesitation, he rattled off, "A father should always be helpful, sweet, and ready to play."

I smiled inside at his innocent comments. Then I realized these are the exact same three things, just in the language of a child.

What would it mean for you to be promised companionship? How would that meet a deep need for you?

What would it mean to you to have a protector?

What would you feel if you knew someone specifically chose YOU? What if someone's eyes sparkled when they saw you for exactly who you are?

Out of these three, which do you feel you desire the most in this season of your life?

Now, we know nothing about the father-daughter relationship between the Samaritan woman and her dad. We do know she had a story to tell of wanting, really wanting, love. Dad or no dad, we know she desperately wanted companionship, protection, and exclusive adoration.

Recall her marriage history and current situation: five different husbands and a live-in lover. My favorite coffee shop in College Station, Texas, used to have a specialized drink—decaf house blend, non-fat milk, and sugar-free. It was called the "Why Bother." You get the drift. This describes the state of the Samaritan. She'd been left empty five times before, even when the relationship was laced with wedding vows. The first five guys had wedding rings; the sixth man just got a key.

Somewhere between calculating how much water to retrieve and avoiding the other women in the town, maybe the cyclical thought loop began in her head. What thoughts may have occupied her mind around this subject of love and relationships? Recall the ideas you jotted down on Day One regarding her thoughts surrounding a feeling of loneliness.

She'd been burned many times. And yet her story was far from over. So here we are. I know many of you already identify with this week to an uncomfortable point. The thought may have crossed your mind: *So this is me, huh? Bound for relational mistakes with no escape and forever thirsty?"*

No.

This bears repeating just in case you glossed over it:

No. Please circle that.

Although she didn't know it fully yet, as love unraveled, this is what the Samaritan woman began to learn that day:

Someone calls me Daughter.

Take a moment to let that sit and *feel that.*

Here's the great news: all three desires are met completely and are yours for the asking. Yes, a fabulous meeting awaits in Heaven. But some of this we were meant to experience even now. Why? Because YOU HAVE A DADDY. A good one. A faithful one who longs to take you where you have always belonged. When you accept this, you will see your dream as a little girl come alive. It's what the Samaritan woman hoped for every time she gave her heart away.

The quest for companionship, protection, and exclusive adoration is not just for those who lacked a positive father influence. It's not just for the chasers. It's also for the missers—those who miss the father they once had.

If this is you, you need to hear something: You have more than your memories.

While we do have the memories, we can also look beyond them as we recognize a constant Daddy companion who is with us today, this very second. The Enemy can also give false messages to the "missers." God offers promises of His presence to silence these thoughts. He wants to relieve your heart with the truth that you still belong to somebody. You are His.

Choose one verse from each section below and write it in the space provided. Then choose one verse from the whole list and literally fall in love with it. My prayer is your heart is so drawn to this that it is no chore at all to memorize. I have no doubt, in Jesus' victorious name, this is exactly what will happen.

Companionship

Exodus 33:11

Romans 8:15

Protection

Psalm 91

2 Chronicles 20:15,17

Isaiah 43:1-4

Proverbs 3:23-24

Exclusive Adoration

    Zephaniah 3:17

    1 John 3:1

    Isaiah 41:8-10

    Song of Solomon 2:4

    Psalm 139:17

P.S. We'll dive into additional information on exclusive adoration tomorrow!

Write the special verse(s) you chose as your special one to start memorizing here:

This is a gift from God to you.

    Here are some tips for memorizing your special verse(s): highlight it, re-write in another place, display it in another place, or tell a friend about this hope.

Go back to the truth statement the woman at the well found in Jesus. Write it here in the space below for yourself. You need to see this truth in black and white. Don't forget to capitalize the "D," for *Daughter*, for it is your name. It's what He calls you, specifically you.

Nightlight/Engraving Question:

Reread the verse you chose today. Psalm 107:20 says, "He sent out his word and healed them; he rescued them from the grave" (NIV). Truly, from His Word, we are heart-healed. Write a short prayer to God, asking Him to make this your new unveiled reality! Be sure to make note of the verse you chose and a segment, if not all, of your prayer in your memory section in the back of the book.

Week 3 Day Four

Take a deep breath and close your eyes. In this busy life, I know I hardly ever stop and take a deep breath. It seems there are too many demands. So I invite you to take a deep breath with me and close your eyes. Try to visualize God. Be as specific as you can as you think about His posture towards you. It is just as important to be specific as being honest. I want you to feel complete freedom to be honest here.

After you open your eyes, describe what you see when you visualize God's posture towards you:

The week before Christmas in 2010, *USA Weekend* published an article entitled, "How Americans Imagine God." Responses ran the gamut. Pastel conversation bubbles filled with the contributing quotes served as floating graphics across two full pages. One woman wrote in, "Standing above the clouds, one arm folded across his chest, the other with his hand on his chin."[11]

For many women, this whole idea of God meeting the emotional needs we have for a father is quite foreign. If the idea of a father leaves a bad taste in your mouth, why would you want to rely on God as Father or call Him by that name? Understandable. If the only "father" we knew had the opposite of godly characteristics, God being a father can be a hard sell.

Not only is God labeled our Father in the Bible, but as infants, our parents are the first "God-images" we see. Psychiatrist Anne Marie Rizzuto is noted for studying this phenomenal process at length. To a newborn, his parents are God. They are sovereign (they decide when and how needs are met). They are bigger. They set the tone for the family (loving, stern, or neglectful). They make decisions. Depending on choices the parents make, can you see how it made sense for us, as young children, to mentally gather our thoughts about God from our parents?

In the columns below, list some characteristics you would use to describe your earthly father as well as your heavenly Father, God. Write what first comes to mind. I'm preaching to myself as I say, "Try not to critique your thoughts. Just write them down!"

My Father	God

What do you notice from what you wrote? Do any characteristics overlap? Differ?

What characteristics do you know in your head as fact, but you question in your heart?

How we actually view God is often quite different from a list of characteristics we might write about Him. For example, we might know, at least on a surface level, God is love. We

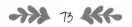

jot it down on our mental or tangible list. But it doesn't touch our hearts because we have a different picture of God.

This can also be difficult because sometimes these promises are in opposition to our experiences. I can tell you one thing for sure: God wants to make you whole in this area. It is God's will for you to know this both in your head and heart.

Sometimes as we carry a sack full of life experiences including disappointments in one hand and a bag full of gifts from God in the other. The Enemy whispers they are both hopeless weights since we cannot merge and make sense of them. But you know what? *Spoiler alert*—God can make sense of these for you, and the second bag eventually overcomes the first. God does not pour out our bag of experience; He doesn't minimize what has happened. He spills the contents of the second over the first, and it eventually impacts everything underneath.

August 24, 2002. I hadn't thought about the date too much until I was thinking about this week's material. Then God brought back the vivid memory of this significant day. The invitation with this date inscribed became a regular part of our home décor. It was proudly displayed in our house for months, leading up to the day of one of my closest high school friend's wedding. The ceremony was simply unforgettable. During the vows, no one in the audience could help but notice how the couple was laughing as they looked at each other. There was no inside joke or funny mishap from the pastor. They were just genuinely overjoyed. Their happiness overflowed into an out loud expression of laughter. Over and over again. The Lord gently told me this is precisely how He looks at you.

Go back with me to a verse from Week One: Day Four, Isaiah 62:5b:

"As a groom rejoices over his bride, so your God will rejoice over you." Sometimes we think God just tolerates us, or that He is a disappointed Father. We have the privilege of knowing that if we are covered in the forgiveness of Christ's blood, we are the perfect bride. Even perfect enough in His sight to—get this—laugh over. Laughter has a way of diffusing anxious thoughts that come with wondering what someone thinks of us, or how he would feel if he "really" knew us. But God knows all of us and smiles a complete smile and laughter of approval. Now close your eyes and imagine that. If you only knew the way He looks at you. And I mean that present tense. My heart is beating so fast as I type this. It's absolutely true, and He can't wait for you to know it.

We see pictures of Jesus with the little children in our church curriculum and in grandiose pictures on the wall. I'm going to be vulnerable with you. I have looked at those pictures before, and said to myself, "I sure *hope* that's true." The pictures portrays everything I would hope Jesus' personality is for me. But is it accurate?

Read the following verses. What pictures of God do you discover are true here? Is it, in fact, accurate? Journal your thoughts in the spaces provided below.

Deuteronomy 1:29-34 (revisit from Week Two)

John 17:22-23

Psalm 103:13

1 John 4:18

In Matthew 7:9-11, we learn He loves us like the best earthly father you've ever encountered or dreamed of—and more. Actually "much more" it says. In Deuteronomy 1:29-31, we see that protection is part of the plan when you have God as a Daddy. Here His very words give us a visual of His carrying us. John 17:22-23 tells us Jesus wants us to be in the close huddle—as close as He is with the Father. He wants us to be in that kind of relationship with Him. From Psalm 103:13, we must never forget He is for us, and He cares deeply. 1 John 4:18 serves as a reminder of, "Oh, yes, I don't need to worry about that." Or an even more powerful, "Perfect love won't let me worry about that."

We can know that it is more than we can dream up in a photo or in our imagination. We can know this as accurate truth. What does it mean to have a Daddy? It means you are the apple of someone's eye (Psalm 17:8, NIV). It means you have unconditional and uncontested favor. It means you have a lap, a refuge, and most importantly a home in the form of a person. And after all, when we get to the bottom of all our desires—isn't this *it*?

Nightlight:

Spend some more time closing your eyes and imagining again the truth of God rejoicing over you as a groom looks at His bride. Imagine an expression of laughter when He looks into your eyes. He knows you and still loves you more than you know. But we're getting closer to knowing . . .

Why You Should Keep Going

Ok, time out. This can be heavy. Some of the false messages you learned from your father are buried deep, and this process hurts. Right now you might want to stop altogether and throw this book into the garage sale pile. But just wait, because if you are reading this, you are already well into the process of victory. If you feel the heat from the Enemy—another false lie that it's just too much—there is no reason to slow down or stop. It's all the more reason to keep going.

While I was writing this book, several bouts of spiritual warfare hit my family. God opened huge doors to get this message out to women, and each time after I had a meeting about teaching or publishing this material, something would happen. After two rounds of the stomach flu back to back, Lysol offering to advertise on my blog, and subsequent upper-respiratory issues at our house, one night my husband looked at me from the couch and wearily (but jokingly) asked, "Can you stop writing this book?" At least, I think he was joking. But we both could see the possibility of this being part of the Enemy's plan to get us down.

Have you ever had a time when you felt like the Enemy tried to stop you from moving the direction God wanted you to go? If not, have you known of this to happen to someone else? (I can think of some people who felt this way in the Bible!)

Even though working through the false messages is a process—I want you to hear something: With the Spirit of God, you absolutely *can* accomplish this. I like what Herbal

Essence puts on the back of their shampoo bottles. I flipped it over the other day and was pleasantly surprised to read this text under what is normally labeled the "directions" section: "YOU KNOW THE DRILL: Keep things smooth with this lush lather by rinsing and repeating." There was just something refreshing about this. They assumed a bit of confidence in me as a consumer. They didn't even stick to the idea of putting the heading of "directions" on the bottle, as if I needed to know how to use shampoo. So it is with this journey. It's a process, but I have God-sized confidence in what He can and will do in your heart if you will let Him. You, too, now know the drill: rinse out the negative, false messages in your head, rinse in truth, and repeat.

FAQ Segment

Q: Sometimes I have a good feeling when I think of God as my Daddy. But then the old feelings come right back—old hurts, memories, or life itself gets in the way of me really thinking about Him being there for me. Am I doing something wrong? Why the back and forth?

> A: Think back to the woman at the well. She had a glorious, "mountain top" experience the day she met Jesus. And yet, she had to go back to her routine. Even though **she met Jesus in person,** I'm sure there were times her past came back to haunt her, certain people remained unfriendly, or she became weighted down with chores of this earth. She was human, too. This back and forth will occur; it does not mean you are doing anything wrong. Continue to tell yourself the truth. Remind yourself of the encounters you have had with Jesus and don't let anyone, not even yourself, tell you they did not happen. Write them down. Highlight the words in your Bible. If the memories remain uncomfortably painful, consider confiding in a strong, Christian friend (I recommend same gender) and/or counselor. This does not mean you are weak. Seeking help from another is a way you can cement the truth in your heart by sharing out loud with another person carrying the Spirit of God. In a safe relationship, this could be another way of God's sharing His love with you.

Week 3 Day Five

*C*hristian psychologist Larry Crabb says the central fear of a woman is that she will not be truly known.[12]

Think about this. Do you agree or disagree with this statement? Why?

I haven't seen any other concept universally "click" with the hearts of women more than this one. From teenagers to adult women of all ages, this statement results in a head and heart nod, often accompanied with tears. *What women really want is for someone to know them fully—the depths of them.*

Just take a look at the population of the blogosphere. People are joining and posting constantly. Bloggers blog in faith. The blogger has faith that someone actually reads about the expanse of what matters to her—from what she has endured and passionately executed to the latest recipe she attempted. The drive of the blogging culture points to the fear of not being known, paralleled with the number one need of being known. With regards to blogging, Bob Walsh shared his interview with futurist Alvin Toffler in 2006, which includes this comment, "I just think America is steeped in loneliness, and that a lot of going online is a way to assuage that loneliness."[13] Consider how this made sense over a decade ago, and how much farther society has gone with this since then. It's only amplified.

Walsh writes about the usefulness of connection through blogging. It's sold as an activity to draw community from an impersonal society. The culture is moving further and further apart, yet people are desperate to touch one another. In a distressing way, the paradox makes sense. People also have a great fear of their biggest desire (being known) because of the false thought that we are dependent on imperfect humans to give this gift to us. So they connect to people through an isolated mechanism in a world where there is no eye contact, no face-to-face, instant reaction from a friend or enemy.

It's been a few days since we've been back in our main text of John 4. We are returning today to the awkward scenario (and remember, this actually happened to this sister) in verses 16-18:

> " 'Go call your husband,' He told her, 'and come back here.'
>
> 'I don't have a husband,' she answered.
>
> "'You have correctly said, 'I don't have a husband,' " Jesus said. "For you've had five husbands, and the man you now have is not your husband. What you have said is true.' "

What do you think she felt in this moment? We don't like to go to the grocery store without makeup. Let's think about the vulnerability level here. What is unique about what happens later in the story? See verses 28-29 and 39-42.

Here's the thing: if the Samaritan woman was painfully uncomfortable (which I do not think she was), it did not last. Jesus had the ability to move her from feeling shamed to feeling known. This was her *takeaway*; it's the very part she told townspeople about her experience: "Come, see a man who told me everything I ever did. Could this be the Messiah?" (v. 29). This was what astounded her the most about her encounter with the Lord.

Truly, He preoccupied her with His promise, and it trumped her problems.

Consider what you have done with your need for someone to know you. I mean really, really know you.

What is your initial emotional response to the idea of being known? Do you love it or fear it? What do you think leads you to feel this way?

Because Someone can. Someone does. And He is absolutely trustworthy with all of it. Earlier this week, each of us learned "Someone calls me Daughter."

Here's the second truth we can know, and that would change our lives if we lived life aware of this:

I am known. Really, really known.

The other day as I was getting my daughter out of the car, she hugged me with her super-toddler strength and said, "Mommy, I love the whole of you!" That touched me so deeply because nothing could be closer to the Gospel.
Read 1 John 3:20 and 1 John 1:9.

In the space provided, rewrite the truth stated above, "I am known. Really, really known," and add to it "Jesus loves the whole of me."

Can you receive that?

I confess, I'm a romantic. As a young woman dreaming of her future mate, I had the perfect scene in mind. I longed for the moment God would place a man in my life to be my forever best friend. Time went on, and the imagined scene grew more specific. An evening complete with a fireplace and fully open hearts. I envisioned telling him everything that would have disqualified me from being the model girlfriend, fiancé, or lifelong mate—yet I would receive unconditional love and acceptance. We would embrace in a larger than life hug and experience romance through forgiveness. At last, he knew it all, and he still loved me. I just couldn't wait for that moment. What relief and what love would arrive.

My imperfections had to await resolution until the day I met "him." This "evening of confession" would occasionally surface in my mind when I recalled my flaws.

When the plans for this fireside romance were finally put down on paper, God distinctly told me, "You've already experienced this, you know." Of course. I had already been forgiven by my beloved Savior. He loved me unconditionally before I failed, after I failed, and while I was failing. The fireside chat took place the day I accepted His gift of the cross, and it happened just as hoped. God wasn't laughing at this "dream." After all, it was not a fantasy. It was a storyline He had already written and completed in full. I didn't have to wait for a man to sweep me off my feet with his forgiveness. God already knew the full scope of my life and willingly loved me.

The Lord distinctly brought me to conviction through this verse in Hosea: "She has not acknowledged that I was the one . . ." (Hosea 2:8, NIV). He was and is *the one*. The fantasy was a dream of having someone know me and still love me after they knew me. God is waiting by the fire for any woman who has this dream.

One of the awesome truths we get to learn about God is He not only understands us in our present and accepts us fully for our past, He was *with us* in our past. He's not a new person who has come on the scene and plays catch up with you about your life. He was there. There's something so special about people we have default history with. They "get it." They were present at the important moments and all the moments in between. You don't have to explain it to them.

Have you ever had a relationship like this? If so, who was it? _____
If you recall, describe the situation when you realized you had this type of relationship. (This may run the gamut from completely hilarious to deeply emotional.)

My grandfather died in 2011. At the visitation, there was a friend who showed up from out of town, and I didn't have to explain anything or anybody to her. This particular friend transcended all of the different people present because she grew up with me. She knew my family, my extended family, and who all of these people were. I'll never forget the thoughtfulness and effort she took to be there that night. She represented someone who knew more than any of my other friends how this death affected the whole family because she knew me so well.

It reminds me of the soul cry in Proverbs 14:10 which says,

"Each heart knows its own bitterness,
and no one else can share its joy" (*NIV*)

What does this verse mean to you?

Again, "*but God.*" While it is true for most human relationships that no one can fully appreciate the level of either our pain or happiness, our Savior completely knows how far our disappointments go and understands the excitements we rejoice over in life. After all, if you have acknowledged Him as Savior, He indwells in your heart and fully cares about every detail of His dwelling. Sometimes I just want someone who "gets me." What would change if we only knew we possessed that?

Think of a current situation you are dealing with that you would feel differently about if you knew you were known in this intimate way?

List specifically what is important to you about each aspect of being known by God.

1. His complete forgiveness of your past

2. His valuing your present (understanding your present emotions, situations)

3. His presence throughout your history

We can be without fear because our need is met. Wherever you are in your day, take this one with you.

Remember the replacement thoughts we left "to be continued" from earlier this week? After studying the Samaritan woman's encounter with Jesus and claiming the promises that God is our Daddy and embracing the concept that we are totally known, we can begin to fill in those blanks.

Recall this was some of the woman's thought summary relating to the feelings of being **unloved and invisible:**

- I am a drain on people; I identify myself in this way.
- I'm invisible, and my voice does not matter.
- I'm a failure in the relationship department.

Her thought summary related to feeling **isolated, lonely,** and **left out:**

- I'm better off alone.
- I must keep this all inside and hide how I really feel.
- The closest I will get to companionship is continuing to chase men.
- I hate being alone, and it will always be this way.

The writer in me desperately wants to believe the woman at the well had a journal handy to process her thoughts after that eventful day. We know she left the well in a hurry. She ran back into the town to tell the people about this man she met. She literally carried the Gospel to the very people with whom she probably feared sharing anything at all! But after she went home, after the dust settled, maybe these were some of the conclusions she wrote on her heart (if not in a rustic, personalized journal from Etsy).

> "He taught me I could trust something new. He put a banner over me that read, 'This one IS worth something.' He loved me like someone who had known me all my life. I'm not just worth something—I was fully cherished today in my moment with Him. I felt safe. I had purpose. I have purpose. He delighted in meeting me. I was and still am part of the plan."

I'm thanking God in advance with you for the unique thought summaries and feelings you will have as you go through this journey.

Every Girl Loves a S.A.L.E.

Week 4 Day One

There was almost nothing pleasant about the day we said goodbye to my grandmother, "Jajo." She was my namesake, my pal. At least I can say it was the perfect weather for a funeral. The sun was out, the sky was bright. When dark clouds and puddles surround loved ones on such a day, it seems to match the emotion too closely. A little natural light never hurts such a dismal experience.

At the gravesite, I saw a little more "light" than I expected. Many familiar people gathered there after the memorial service, but one stranger stood out. Striking, bright red hair framed her face just the shade of my grandmother's. The 30-something woman solemnly approached me in her business suit, tissue in hand. She shook her head in despair, "She was like a mother to me . . ." She was sobbing. *Umm, who are you?* At the time, I was quite possessive of my grandmother and didn't want to share her with such an outsider who thought she was a daughter. As she introduced herself, suddenly this tearful woman became dear to my heart. She was the manager of Stein Mart. Yes, Stein Mart, an American retail playground for fashionistas like Jajo. My grandmother spent countless hours in her department store. I had heard stories about this manager, how she hosted private after-hours shopping events exclusively for my grandmother and her friends. Oh my. I was grieving at the grave with the manager of Stein Mart. Again, at the graveside, people! The setting where traditionally only the closest family and friends attend and comfort one another. But I wasn't complaining; the moment served as a much-appreciated comic relief.

Though not every girl loves to shop like my grandmother, everyone has interests. Every girl loves a sale. Whether it's concert tickets, outdoor recreational equipment, dishes, music or eye liner, when "your thing" is on sale, it's a thrill. In the S.A.L.E portion of our study, we will discuss four practical steps to make this life of promise an actual lifestyle. While we all may naturally desire this lifestyle of anticipation we've been talking about, the irony is how unnatural it seems to obtain. So what's next? What about the days we just aren't feeling it? (I'm sure the woman at the well had this human thought.)

Each letter in the S.A.L.E. acronym represents a practical step in this process. These four key ingredients are the exact ones God has used in my own spiritual valleys and with other women I've been privileged to journey with through the years. They moved the idea of experiencing God from desire to reality.

Our first action point in the "S.A.L.E." process is:

Go ahead and Stamp it as Truth

Read John 4:46-54, a story about a royal official who was desperate for Jesus to heal his son.

After you read the story, go back to verse 50. Two significant things happen. What does Jesus do? What does the man do?

He could have kept begging to make "sure" Jesus would do as He said. Anyone else reading this like me and likes to "check" if Jesus is good on a promise? (Not good or necessary, by the way).

He could have asked for a sign or a receipt of the miracle. Something to commemorate there really had been a transaction. All he had was Jesus' word—His only, yet fully valid, confirmation. And yet, *he started home.* This is a miracle in the story itself. He literally had the faith to turn his back on Jesus and walk the other way, as if to say, "Ok, then. Your word is all I needed."

The official believed before he saw his son healed. He believed before he could see life in his son with his own eyes. The Bible says it was the next day before the father made it home. That means he had to go through the entire darkness of night with his thoughts on the events of the day.

How do we see the kindness of God in verse 51?

What is significant to you about what happened in verse 51?

Confirmation literally met the man on his way home the following day. One of the official's servants stopped him with the glad news: his son was better and would live. The two men exchanged information about the exact hour the boy improved. It was the precise time Jesus spoke the words, "Go. Your son will live." God tested the man's faith to a certain point. Then He decided to make the father wait no more. The tenderness of God.

There's a pull in many of us to have faith like this man. But what is our typical human response? We ask for God to work, and even when He gives us His word about a matter, we dance around the topic. Worried. Like the conversation with Him never happened. Unmoved. The truth of the royal official's story addresses just this: There's a time for praying, *begging* even, and then there's a time for believing and *walking*.

Sometimes I feel stuck on certain issues. (My husband would insert here a "You think?" with a full belly laugh.) The Bible tells us to pray without ceasing, but there should be faith in our prayers as well. If we truly are casting our cares on the Lord, believing He cares for us (1 Peter 5:7), then we really should be walking it out like the royal official. In those times I feel like God has told me to go ahead and believe something and I continually wring my hands over the problem, I picture myself on a treadmill. I've tricked myself into thinking I am actually getting somewhere, but I'm really on the same few feet of rubber over and over again. In contrast, I desire to be on a people mover like they have at airports—where you can glide in grace, letting something else carry the load without wasted self-effort.

What is one truth of God you feel like you are on a "people mover" with?

What is a truth or promise He has told you about a certain situation and you are now supposed to take it with you as you "go home" like the royal official? What do you need to go ahead and believe? This will be your Engraving Question for the week, so please rerecord in the back on the reserved page. (It will be a treat to write it twice).

Put your book beside your bed so you won't forget your Nightlight!

Nightlight:

I just continue to marvel at the faith of that guy from John 4:46! Consider the faith of the father in this story and write a prayer for your faith to be like his.

Hunter was 22-months-old when he came down with his first terrible bout with croup. It was September, earlier than we expected cold and flu season to visit the Strong house. The little tot just felt awful. His body rejected the steroids, which brought worse side effects instead of the promised respite. But whether he was in tears or in a moment of reprieve, he continually repeated one phrase. Sometimes I'd hear him say it quietly when he was playing Mega blocks in the other room all by himself, "Mommy Get-Choo. Mommy Get-Choo. Mommy Get-Choo." It wasn't long before I knew exactly where this term originated. He was rehearsing the one thing he heard me promise him all his life: "Mommy's got you." It was all he could muster up to say, but it was enough. It satisfied him.

Said with such conviction and heart, it was as if he had to believe it. The saying somewhat grounded him when his world stood upside down. In my arms or in another room, amidst all else, at least he knew "Mommy Get-Choo" remained true.

This is what it means to "Stamp it as Truth." Inevitably, Hunter would say this whether he was feeling ill *or* better. He said it with the same inflection and expectation. There's a lesson in this. Just like Hunter lobbed out the phrase he heard all his little life, we can label God's Word with a bright red stamp as the absolute truth even before we "feel" the consolation of it. When we rehearse what God has told us over and over in our head, when we return to those verses that seem just like words on a page at times, we can claim comfort. This includes the comfort in both our happiest of moments and in our sick Septembers.

We have adult forms of "sick Septembers." We may have outgrown croup, but we haven't outgrown the need for comfort in our crisis.

How would you fill in the blank? What would you name it right now in your stage of life? When we return to those verses and rehearse them, we can claim comfort in our happiest of moments and in our _____

_____ .

I went through what I would describe as a "soul earthquake" during a particular season of my life. This term came from a direct quote from one of my journals, and it certainly was an accurate description. Although there have been more than one of these earthquakes, this particular trembling of my world happened when I entered college. There I was, excited to take in my first breath of university life, yet leaving everything I knew to encounter everything I didn't. I had so much to be elated about, but it was such a change to be away from home. During orientation week, the new students learned a slogan that captured the unique quality of our university: "The women are strong, and the guys aren't afraid to hug each other." It really was like family. I was all over the traditions, the friends, the bonding, the football games, and dances. The new social life, leadership, and activities were enough to keep anyone busy and in community.

Yet, in the pit of my stomach, I was so lonely.

When I encountered any downtime from fun activities or study pressures, when I was given a second to *think*, I was a mess. And boy, does the Enemy know what a thinker I am.

Day after day, in personal Bible study, God offered His security. But I still longed for my physical home. During my tenure at the University of Mary Hardin-Baylor, we had chances to feed our souls with spiritual truth pretty much around the clock. It wasn't forced, but if you sought it out, it was certainly there. Sometimes I took the bait and allowed Satan's lies to come in to my heart about my loneliness, which made me feel awkward when I participated in the Christian activities. At times like this, I pictured everyone around me as spiritually "better." *They don't seem homesick. They are content.* I went to on-campus Bible studies and envied what seemed to be the peaceful worship of my peers while mine felt like a wrestling match. Even though the deepest part of me desired to be at the events, I became weary of this game. Being homesick wasn't the only problem anymore; the Enemy's schemes spiraling from my lonely feelings desperately drained my spirit.

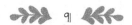

Once again, I see the powerful foothold of our thought life, as the attacks came via this route. The Enemy attacked with doubts of salvation. *If you were a real Christian, you would love to attend revivals and Bible studies, wouldn't you?* And so the spiral continued. *And if you don't have salvation, you really have no one. You thought God was the only one you came here with, and now you don't even have Him. Aren't there tons of Bible verses talking about the plight of an unbeliever like you?* He loves kicking us while we're down.

However, if you were to peruse through my journals from college, you might think I was on a retreat or a soul vacation instead of experiencing an earthquake. Here's one example where simultaneous scenes in life come into play. The Hero of my story was still working in me at the exact same time I was going through my wrestling match. Yet my journals recounted themes of promise and dose after dose of daily medicine through Scripture. The paradox amazes me. This was one of the hardest times of my life and yet, my words, page after page, literally sing a continuous song of hope. It doesn't make sense because the words didn't appear to match the internal struggle. Except that I knew the source of my joy would eventually be found in Him. **He assured me there is no victory where there is no battle.**

I told myself the truth from 2 Timothy 1:12:

"*. . . I know the One I have believed in and am persuaded that He is able to guard what has been entrusted to me until that day.*"

What are the three action words from Paul in this verse?

What is God's action according to this verse?

So I kept tapping in. I kept calling out to the One I knew though could not feel. I kept writing what I knew was truth until the hope of eventually turned into finally.

Taped up in an envelope, hidden in the middle of the journal from freshman year, is a 12-page letter I wrote to God. While writing this week, I opened it for the first time. Raw emotion emerged as I carefully unfolded the pages formerly sealed for so many years. My heartache, confusions, and statements of what I *knew* to be true (although I didn't always feel it) ended on page 12 as "Abba. Abba. Abba. Thank You for listening. You will answer my prayer and have been alongside me this whole time." Believing these written words was a step forward, but it definitely didn't mean I had it all together. The act of going ahead and believing repeatedly, like the dedicated footsteps of a marathon runner on pavement, was a vital component to regaining life from a weighed-down spirit.

I see this truth come full circle again through my son as a toddler. When my 15-month-old, Lego®-loving Hunter played with his blocks and reached a stack he just wasn't quite strong enough to pull apart, he would run across the room saying, "Helper! Helper!" I couldn't help but stop everything and respond. I don't know where he picked it up, but he asked for "helper" instead of just "help" when he needed assistance with his all-important play. He called me by a name he counted on me to uphold. This absolutely touches the heart of God when we call out to Him. As Abba. Savior. Holder of our burdens. Comforter.

Helper.

Not that it makes God any more of a refuge, helper, or savior than He already is to us when we call out to Him; He is already 100% of those names. But it conditions our hearts and minds as an absolute resistance to the Enemy and an anchor in the quake.

Flip back through previous pages. Based on what you've discovered so far in the study, what name of God can you call out for right now? Will you decide to put this name on repeat?

I tell my kids, "We'll go on a treasure hunt for it" anytime they lose something. Here are some ideas if you need suggested places to look for your treasure of who God is to you: (Psalm 32:7, Psalm 68:5, Isaiah 33:6, Hebrews 13:5, Isaiah 43:4, Isaiah 33:6).

Take a few moments and let's practice. In Week Three, we coached the woman at the well on her thoughts and feelings. Now we will try it for ourselves. God has armed us with much truth lately. Flip back through your pages, pull from Scriptures you've discovered, and insert here for our Replacement Thoughts section.

Emotion:

Situation:

Possible Thought Chain:

Specific Thought Summary (brief, bullet points):

Replacement Thoughts:

Go ahead, friend. STAMP this as TRUTH, and know His heart responds.

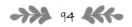

 **Week 4** **Day Three**

I'm a planner by personality. When practiced in the Spirit, this is a strength, but when this turns into control issues, it's a personality flaw. I like to know how everything will turn out in the end whether it's a trivial social event or a crucial family decision. But God certainly did not call us to know everything. Shadrach, Meshach and Abednego (we'll call them S, M, & A) provide a practical example of how to believe even before all the questions are answered. It works almost every time to bring the peace that passes understanding in a situation of waiting. Aren't we in a situation of waiting if we choose to believe before we feel it?

King Nebuchadnezzar ruled at the time of S, M & A's awesome story. Read Daniel 3:1-12.

What did the king do? What was his decree?

According to verse 7, who does it say fell down to worship?

Well, S, M, & A weren't all about this, as we find out in verse 12. They ignored the law and went on to praise the one and *only* God. This sounds like a pretty noble response, but it

gets even better when we realize they were threatened. They were not only breaking the law of the king; they were knowingly breaking a law they knew would cost them a trip to the fiery furnace if disobeyed. The king found out about the guys' decision and confronted them.

According to verses 13-15, summarize the king's response to S, M & A:

Here's what they said back to King Nebuchadnezzar:

"Shadrach, Meshach and Abednego replied to him, 'King Nebuchadnezzar, we do not need to defend ourselves before you in this matter. If we are thrown into the blazing furnace, the God we serve is able to save us from it, and he will deliver us from your Majesty's hand. But even if he does not, we want you to know, Your Majesty, that we will not serve your gods or worship the image of gold you have set up.'" (Daniel 3:16-18, NIV).

Write out the six words that appear **after** "and he will deliver us from your Majesty's hand":

"_____ . . ."

This is going to be a new phrase for us, called the S.M.A. Principle. What would it be like if God (or our enemy for that matter) caught us saying this when we don't have the answers to the end of our stories? "But even if he does not . . ." Try it out with a situation you are either currently facing or fear will come in the future. This is useful for many issues that can paralyze us throughout life if left to our own "what if" whirlwinds. For example, parenting can bring up all kinds of these questions inside me. What about the struggles Hunter will face at school? The temptations? The words and images he might be exposed to but is sheltered from now? What happens when my son learns how to drive and he's used to an iPhone entertaining him as he drives down the road? What if my daughter thinks she is in love at an early age with a guy who is wrong for her?

Three heroes gave such a beautiful faith picture of what we can put in our minds. They said, "We know God is able. No problem for Him. But even if He does not save us from this drama, He's still worth saving all our love for."

The S.M.A. Principle goes like this: Confidently claim you know what God is able to do. But we can't stop here. If we only go this far, we can go off on a rabbit trail of "but what if He doesn't . . . " and find ourselves caught in worries instead of finishing the statement with the guarantee we *do* have. We have to finish like the boys facing the furnace, "But even if He does not . . . " and fill in the blank with the platform on which we set our hearts.

Let's try this together. Think of a "what if" rabbit trail you've had on your mind lately.

Yes, that's a good example. If you're like me, I knew it wouldn't take you long to come up with one.

Using S, M, & A's response as a template, use your story to change their response to your personal response:

1. If we are/I am _____ ("thrown into the blazing furnace," v. 17).
2. God is able to _____
3. But even if He does not, _____ (your action)

Just like we can't stop with the first six words, the story of S, M, & A didn't stop there either (find the rest of their story at the end of Daniel Chapter 3). But what the six-word catch phrase will do is give us a running start towards thinking outside of our natural mentality.

I love the fact the people in the Bible are real. Although the woman at the well had a crazy, awesome experience with God Himself, where did she go after the fact (review John 4:28-30)?

The woman had to go back to real life and reenter her town after she met Jesus. Her story does not have an Enoch-ending; she does not spend time with Jesus and is then miraculously whisked away from her non-committal boyfriend and the town gossips. But going back into town after the encounter with Jesus? We can identify with this. After intimacy with the King, we all have to go back into our town.

You have spent time reading about this focus on God that takes your heart to a new place. Sooner or later—you'll not be reading this book, and life will call you back into town—back to your real life. You'll have to navigate, with the help of the Holy Spirit, how these truths you have discovered are transported into your real world.

From what we know in the biblical text, the Samaritan woman did it. She went back, willingly faced the people, and shared about her experience. The Bible does not go into detail about how she handled it in the days to come. Even though many in the town believed, I imagine she still had to endure judgment from some unfriendly peers and maybe a lack of uplifting words from her guy. What did she do then? Her life is a good example of a heart needing to anticipate Jesus' promise for a future security as well as a current hiding place.

When Jesus left the Samaritan woman's physical sight, she had to believe. When she found herself fighting depressed feelings at night and she asked if her encounter with Jesus really even happened, she had to have faith. She had to know in her soul she had an irreversible stamp of authenticity despite her feelings.

"Jesus replied, 'If you only knew the gift God has for you and who you are speaking to, you would ask me, and I would give you living water'" (John 4:10, NLT).

"Money can't buy happiness, but it can buy marshmallows, which is kinda the same thing." No phrase merited more placement stamped on a burlap pillow at the time than that one. You couldn't tell me anything truer. You just as well could have said Blue Bell® ice cream is the best (also true) or July in Texas is hot. I was the mom of a little boy who would do anything for one of those white, chubby cylinders—the proverbial Klondike bar. The importance of marshmallows is one of many, many lessons God has taught me through my son. Not the least of these being God's generous desire for faith of a child. We've lived it, I've witnessed it, and my five-year-old son leapt into it. *The simplicity of salvation.*

Hearing my son ask Jesus into his heart was one of the best days of my life. Knowing his sincerity, his simple understanding, his wanting to have God forgive him and live in his heart was but a grain of sand compared to how willing God was to permanently indwell in him. I know that. And it was wonderful to relive it again for myself. If you've struggled with doubt in your salvation, I pray this week will be the point at which "The God of peace will soon crush Satan under your feet" (Romans 16:20).

Even though money can't buy happiness, I know happiness can be bought. Yes, that's right. ***Happiness can be bought.***

It's actually biblical! What does 1 Peter 1:18-19 say about this?

Our chance at happiness was bought for us at the cross. This was the reason Jesus knew he could offer a better life and living water to the woman. This is why he can offer abundant life to us. **Because someone loved us enough to purchase life for us, this is our joy and happiness.** When you know someone loved you enough to literally give his life for you, it changes how you think and feel. Jesus explained to the woman, "If you only knew the gift God has for you and who you are speaking to, you would ask me, and I would give you living water" (John 4:10, NLT).

Our second action point in the S.A.L.E process is:

Ask.

Why does God tell us to ask? It is not just one more step to "do." Today and tomorrow, we will see four aspects of asking and what God does in the process. You'll be so thankful this is part of the plan.

First of all, ___asking is about relationship___.

Simply put, asking implies the bond of a relationship. Just think about how God created an infant to give cues to his or her mother. The way the infant does his asking is to cry, and the way beautiful trust is built between caregiver and child is through the continual asking and giving process between the two individuals. God designed it this way; the infant expresses a need, and the parent gives. The asking process starts at the first breath of life.

When the trust continues to grow between two people, the asking naturally multiplies. Just think of the six- or seven-year-olds you know who can't stop asking questions. Relationship and joy are by-products of habitual asking.

Secondly, ___when we know WHO we are asking, we ask confidently.___

There must have been something different about Jesus. He made the Samaritan feel vulnerable enough to share instead of feeling threatened. She was excited to be known instead of being shamed, and now she trusted instead of feeling too skeptical to ask for His water.

Think of a time you asked for something and the person may not have been trustworthy. Do you think you ever subconsciously put this person's "face" on Jesus and expect Him to treat you the same way? Circle one.

Yes   *No*

What does Hebrews 4:14-16 tell us about who we are asking? What specifics does God want us to know about approaching Him?

Also, take in the richness of Matthew 7:9-11:

"What man among you, if his son asks him for bread, will give him a stone? Or if he asks for a fish, will give him a snake? If you then, who are evil, know how to give good gifts to your children, how much more will your Father in heaven give good gifts to those who ask Him!"

Almost the exact same passage is recorded in Luke 11. What difference do you notice about the Luke passage, specifically in verse 13?

Not only is He in the position as a wonderful Father to give good gifts, He will also give the Holy Spirit. God wants us to get the point. Of course, he is ready and waiting to give you the ultimate gift of the Spirit as soon as we ask. He paved the way with His sacrifice. He will never reject our asking for a relationship with Him. It was never meant to be a tricky path.

Here's something else we can know about the "who" we are asking: He believes in you more than you believe in yourself. You never have to hesitate when that's the case. Look at Luke 1:3. Who was one of the people to whom Luke was writing his book?

He plays a small role, but because of what God showed me through this passage, "Theo" has become a new favorite Bible character. My study Bible states Theophilus was most likely identified as an acquaintance of Luke's who was driven to know more about this idea of Jesus. The footnote on this passage specifically describes Theophilus as having a "strong interest" in Christianity. And yet, the commentary also tells us the name Theophilus means "one who loves God."[14] There's a parallel but also a significant gap between interest and love. This is a prime example of how God understands the end of our story differently than we do. From beginning to end, He has a different vision for your life. Because, you see, God gave Theophilus his name before he loved God. If this was his birth name, he was named this before he even took up this "strong interest." *God sees who we are before we are.*

How does that invigorate you—to know that you can come to someone who sees both who you are now and at the finish line? Journal your thoughts here.

Week 4 Day Five

Yesterday we learned asking is about relationship and that when we know "who" we are asking, it makes all the difference. We learned characteristics about Jesus that silenced any anxiety about asking; in fact, we traded anxiety for bold confidence.

The next lesson we can learn about asking is in ***recognizing a need*** and ***finding refreshment.***

I always enjoy reflecting on my pastor's commentary on our longing for heaven. Sometimes he'll compare it to having a glass of iced tea after a full summer day in the Texas heat. Just like our toil here on earth only makes us long that much more for heaven, iced tea tastes more refreshing when accompanied by pink cheeks and beads of sweat on the brow.

Sometimes when life is going smoothly, I wonder if I would be more grateful for the present circumstances if I had a picture of what might have been. In the spiritual realm, God can give us glimpses of life without Him, but anything more than a glimpse would be like sitting down to watch a horror film. Complete torture. Taking a serious look at what God has told us in His Word about life without Him is important. Reading about this will be no more than we can handle, so do not fear. It will serve as a reality check for us. An opportunity to see the drought without the living water. Jesus gives us a story beginning in Luke 16:19 describing the contrast between the life of one who truly believes in Christ and the "agony" and "torment" of the one who does not.

What is an example of something you appreciated so much more after you realized your need for it?

If you have never accepted Christ before, just like He was excited to reveal Himself to the Samaritan woman, He is more than ready for you to ask and receive. The gift is ready. He wants you to *recognize* what He has saved you from, *ask* Him for forgiveness of your wrongs, and *receive* the celebration He gives of a life with Him. As we take this journey on how to live mindful of God's truths, this section will make or break your ability to live this. Because it's not about your ability. It's about asking for His unfailing Spirit's ability to live in you.

We have to first accept that our happiness is bought; then it can be thought.

If we don't acknowledge this, we are unable to think and live a new lifestyle conscious of the gift like we have discussed.

Take time to read the following verses, praying for God to bring light to what needs clarity:

"For all have sinned and fall short of the glory of God" (Romans 3:23). *We've all messed up. No one is "closer" to heaven because of what they did or didn't do. None of us are perfect enough to get there. The Samaritan woman's peers weren't better off in God's eyes because they had only been married once or twice. We've all done wrong in some way. We must recognize this to see how far we are from the mark and the height He desires to take us to!*

"For the wages of sin is death, but the gift of God is eternal life in Christ Jesus our Lord" (Romans 6:23).

"He was delivered over to death for our sins and was raised to life for our justification" (Romans 4:25, NIV). *God could not have us walk with Him (on Earth or Heaven) because of our sin. Since we were helpless in our wrongs, God sent His own Son to be the atonement for the death to which we were doomed. This was His greatest act of love.*

"But God proves His own love for us in that while we were still sinners, Christ died for us!" (Romans 5:8). *This is a most heart-gripping fact. Again, note His vision for us from beginning to end. God loved us when we were deliberately far from His ways, and so unloving toward Him. His vision out of love for us exceeded our sin.*

"If we confess our sins, He is faithful and righteous to forgive us our sins and to cleanse us from all unrighteousness" (1 John 1:9).

"If you confess with your mouth, 'Jesus is Lord,' and believe in your heart that God raised Him from the dead, you will be saved" (Romans 10:9). *He didn't stay dead. This is the most important aspect of our faith. Because He didn't stay in the grave, neither do we. He rose from the dead and lives. He forever defeated all that binds us.*

Yesterday, we talked about the expectancy we have when we ask a person for something. We trust they will handle our request with care. In the case of Jesus offering the living water, we can trust He will do as He said.

One promise of this is found in 2 Corinthians 1:20a. What does it say?

All these promises are YES when we have Christ. And when do we have Christ? As the verses state above, as soon as you believe in Him as Lord and Savior from your sins. And then there's never a way it can be taken away from you.

Read 2 Corinthians 1:21-22 below.

> *"Now it is God who makes both us and you stand firm in Christ. He anointed us, set his seal of ownership on us, and put his Spirit in our hearts as a deposit,* **guaranteeing** *what is to come"* (NIV, [emphasis mine]).

What assurance are we given here?

Highlight, rewrite, or make notes in the margin of what is meaningful about this promise to you.

You can be sure of this. You can also be sure I have this one underlined with red stars marching all around this verse in my Bible.

Asking in full view of what God has done for us not only increases our appreciation—but also our love. The Bible says a person who realizes how much they have been forgiven has a bottomless love for God. In contrast, the person who thinks he has no need or has only been forgiven a little bit only slightly loves God (see Luke 7:47). I don't know about you, but I want to be in love with God with an outrageous love.

What is one thing God has forgiven you from that causes you to "love Him much" as we read in Luke 7:47? **Think on this throughout today, dwelling on the depth of His love for you.**

Lastly, we learn how asking means **_we are not in control._**

This might sound scary at first glance. But in a control-obsessed culture, when a vacation is defined by turning off every controlling electronic device constantly scheduling and rescheduling our worlds with alerts and distractions, let's find rest with this point.

Throughout this study, we've learned many tips and things that help us stay focused on what God has for us. We've talked about how to be proactive in our fight against the Enemy.

But it's not all about what *we do*. We should all feel like we lightened our load by a few tons. If we forget we are meant to ask for this abundant life to be possible, we are still holding on to an unnecessary burden. How often do we "try, try, try" and "do, do, and do more" instead of "asking" or just "being" in Him? We are to be at Jesus' feet, taking His hand and asking for Him to help us make our emotions and minds whole. Why? Because He is the Who we are talking to, and He's eager to do just that. When we learn of His precious purchase for us . . .

All we have to do is ask. Really.

"Ask and it will be given to you" (Matthew 7:7, niv)

Nightlight:

Have you asked Jesus to save you from your sins and give you new, eternal life in Him? If not, and you want that, here's how you ask. Just like in the verses you read earlier, you pray these ideas (it does not have to be these exact words) from your heart.

Dear Father in Heaven,

I know I am a sinner. I know my sin separates me from You. I confess I have done wrong and desire to turn from it. Thank YOU for making a way to have permanent forgiveness and be with You forever. That way was costly to You, as I believe in Your death on the cross for my sins. I also believe that You rose from the dead and now live. Please live in me now, and help me as I turn from my sins and live totally for You. You are my Lord, and I will never find a better love.

In Jesus' wonderful name I pray, Amen.

If you are already a believer, rejoice in God's plan that it's all yours for the ASKING.

Week 5

For You to Experience

Week 5 · Day One

" 'You will seek Me and find Me when you search for Me with all your heart. I will be found by you'—this is the Lord's declaration."

JEREMIAH 29:13-14

Let's review and list our first two action points in the S.A.L.E. process:

_____

_____

Our third action is:

Look on Purpose.

When I look back through my journal pages to my time of turbulence during college, I am amazed at the sheer volume of writing that took place over those years. Many Christians say times of crisis often make us stay on our knees. In my case, I'm surprised my stomach didn't have permanent imprints of my dorm comforter because of the hours I spent lying in bed, leaning over my pen and Bible.

When you're in a time of trial, you can "stamp it as truth" as long as possible, but when Satan is steadily trying to feed you lies, you reach a point where you run low on ammo. I stamped what I knew to be true and called out to the God I knew was real, but more evidence was needed to put it in my heart. When your stamper runs out of ink, the Spirit will urge you to seek for more truth.

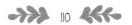

In retrospect, I see how this was the natural progression of my healing. I was like a squirrel gathering her nuts. What else could I find to feed my battling soul? What else? What else? What else? This might come across as enthusiasm, but rest assured, it was a pure hybrid of eagerness and desperation. I had to keep looking.

When it was time to give my stomach and back a break, I glanced in the bathroom mirror framed with that infamous Pepto Bismol pink sheetrock our girls' dorm was known for, and headed out. I was ready once again to face the day. Armed. My heart primed, sometimes timidly, to put what I learned to work. It was a daily sandwich of believing, learning, and believing again.

Leaving my dorm room, I felt armed but also in love. You start to see what you love everywhere. What you habitually daydream about becomes almost like a magnet to your eyes.

Give an example of a time when something was important to your heart, and you started to see it everywhere. (This absolutely can be, but does not have to be a serious example. You know we've all had some trivial heart tugs!)

Two times in college I took specific note of a sparrow flying through the almost cloudless blue sky. Read Matthew 10:29-31. What heart connection do you think God made for me as I read this? If you were me, what would you have concluded?

When *Finding Nemo* came to the movie theaters, I went with Josh and my girlfriend, Brooke. No children, just three adults enjoying the newest Disney animated movie. The script was quite humorous, but personally, I was fascinated on another level. In that same season, I was reading through the Psalms, specifically chapter 104. As the large screen filled with the invigorating exhibit of marine life, I thought of what I had just read in Psalm 104:25, "Here is the sea, vast and wide, teeming with creatures beyond number—living things both large and small." I don't think I had this verse actually memorized, but in my heart, I was led to worship because I had an idea of what I read just days before. Entertainment was mixed with childlike awe, and it was fun. But I would not have known these verses if I wasn't looking on purpose and seeking with fervor. My journal pages also would have been much emptier. I'm not trying to over-spiritualize things. This is just what happens when you decide your spiritual life and your regular life do not have to be mutually exclusive.

There's a whole dimension of life we'll miss if we don't ask God to open our spiritual eyes. The story found in 2 Kings 6:8-23 helps us understand this idea of looking with intention.

Read the story, and then we'll discuss some key facts.

Who were the people of God at war with?

Why was the enemy king upset? What kept happening according to verses 8-12? (This is actually quite humorous if you think about it).

What did Elisha say in verse 16 and what did he pray in verse 17?

What application can you make with this true story right now in your own life?

He saw something totally different than the servant. Elisha then prayed for God to open the servant's eyes. To my knowledge, the servant already had eyes and probably knew how to count. But Elisha meant for him to see with eyes beyond the ordinary. The Lord answered his prayer. Then the servant saw what he did not see before—he saw what Elisha saw: hills blanketed with horses and chariots. The heavenly army had arrived.

The servant's eyes were opened, but what did the Lord do in verses 18-19?

A similar spiritual application can be taken from a legend about a young, Cherokee Indian boy and his rite of passage. As the tradition goes, the Cherokee boy's father led the young lad into the forest. To become a real man, he had to sit on a stump, blindfolded, all alone and all night. He had to sit it out until he could feel the peek of morning sun. He was not allowed to call for help and forbidden to share the experience with his friends. Dark hour after hour, he sat in complete silence. Silence of any human, that is. There were plenty of frightening sounds—wild creatures and wind, not to mention the haunting voice in his adolescent head of pure vulnerability. Finally, the sun rose. When the boy took off his blindfold, he was shocked to see another pair of legs on a stump directly across from him:

His father's. *He had been there the whole night.* From dark till dawn, he had watched over his son. I cannot help but think of our study's key theme from what Jesus told the woman at the well, "If you only knew . . ."

You and I are a little mix of Elisha's servant, the Arameans and the Indian boy. If you are a believer, you are on the winning side of the army like Elisha's servant, with the ability to have spiritual sight and insight. We might not be in a situation of physical blindness like the Arameans, but we are often blinded to the fact that there's more because our eyes don't make it to the hills or even imagine there is anything on the hills to see. And a lot of the time we're like the little boy on the stump. We are fearful and unaware of the security closer than six inches from us.

Which character do you identify with the most: Elisha, his servant, the Aramean army or the young Cherokee? Is this different from whom you aspire to be? If yes, list who and what needs to change in order for you to see with that perspective?

Week 5 Day Two

God wants you to look at your days with a new set of eyes. Eyes looking beyond the daily distractions and routine. Eyes that look for Him and see the world around us as full of opportunity to experience Him. To do this, we must desire to look further than the tunnel vision our earthly eyes provide for us and enter into imagination. I'm not talking about something mystically weird. This is about taking God's promise of His presence and living your life like He really is on that stump next to you. We may be a little out of practice.

The night Josh and I put together Hunter's crib and dresser for his nursery, we emptied one of the huge boxes and haphazardly threw it into the hallway. Josh quickly commented, "Now if we still had imagination, we would be playing in that right now." We laughed . . . how true.

It is important to distinguish this kind of faith imagination from make-believe and pretending. In this case, they're direct opposites. When we live life with tunnel vision blinders, we don't see things for how they really are. The truth is, we really *are* in a dynamic relationship. We really *are* in a world where opportunities surround us, allowing us to walk in step with the Hero of the story and influence the person next to you for Him. We really *are* given a manual, giving us a myriad of colorful promises we could start collecting in a hybrid of honor and humility in our minds today. The challenge is to believe in something very real, which we are invited to be part of, even though it is not right in front of our eyes.

How does this shape our worldview if we begin to live this way?

My daughter, Paisley, just sees the world differently. She was not taught these things; it's the way she sees life. For example, one afternoon she fell down at the park. Seeing blood and not knowing what to inspect, I asked her where she hurt. She said through tears, "Mommy, I hurt my smiley face," as she pointed to her mouth. Not too long after that, she hurt herself again, and she pointed to her eyebrow—"Mommy, I hurt my rainbow!" It sure is hard to keep from laughing sometimes. When she steps on something hard, she says it's her "high heel" that hurts, and when she touches her Daddy's unshaven "vacation" chin, she says she likes his "sparkles." What a worldview. All of us can probably name someone who just sees the world a little differently. What if . . . in a good, pure, spiritual sense, *we* could be that person? What if we could begin to lift the faith of others, inspiring them to see with this kind of vision?

What does Hebrews 11:1 have to say about what our faith should be?

As the late beloved ministry leader, Dave Busby, said, "Faith demands a leap that our rational minds cannot make."[15] It almost feels soothing and easier to accept to have faith defined in this way. It's ok that it's hard. It's ok that it feels impossible sometimes and unknown because it is.

Do you have an example of a time when you have made this leap?

Like the quote suggests, sometimes this feels impossible in our human brains. Recall who is able to help us with this leap. List a Scripture reference with one such promise if you know one. (And if not, leave it blank, and a friend can help you find one!)

I love what Psalm 119:130 says:

"The unfolding of your words gives light;
it gives understanding to the simple" (NIV)

"Break open your words, let the light shine out
let ordinary people see the meaning" (MSG)

Looking back over yesterday and today's lesson, how is our ability to imagine with faith directly impacted by how earnestly we "look" into the Word of God?

Introduced in Week One, theologican Francis Schaeffer further distinguished faith-imagination from unreality when he said, "All the reality of Christianity rests upon the reality of the existence of a personal God, and the reality of the supernatural view of the total universe."[16]

Schaeffer also brings up an interesting point about our natural worldview when we read the Bible. He suggests we often forget that the miracles of Jesus occurred in real time. For example, he mentions that after the transfiguration, real life occurred again.[17]

Is there a Bible story you believe is true, but it has been a while since you thought how this actually happened on this earth, among real human beings just like yourself?

Last year (ironically on Father's Day weekend), America sentimentally swooned when the house where *Father of the Bride* was filmed went on the market. And yes, the package included *the* basketball goal. The thrill of this going on sale is the prospect of someone actually having the chance to live and walk (and dribble) where these things happened in the movie.

Flip back for a second to pages 104-106 and refresh yourself on the verses. As you read these, I ask the Holy Spirit to open your eyes to what He showed me. These verses, so full of life and promise, are literally our *Father of the Bride* set. He revealed to me it was better than 500 N. Almansor Street in California, not to mention that I already owned it. The verses listed in the last day we studied "Asking," serve as the set where God became my Father. Where He displayed His love for me. Where He showed tears, affection and adoration. Where He didn't want to see me go. The place where my memories began at the cross. When the sin became permanently forgotten and the good memories are what He remembers. By His mercy, I get to walk in this, with Him, every day.

The story of the woman at the well occurred in real time. There was a real day when that actually happened. The supernatural occurred in the same time and space as real, breathing, people with flesh. And likewise, God's power and friendship is closer than we often think. It was meant to transcend and intersect our days. God made it possible to not merely be "close" to us, but to dwell inside us. If we believe God's promises are working even when we cannot see them, and if we are the main characters just a few "leaps" from life-changing truth, the faith imagination can run wild.

Go ahead and read the Nightlight section below. Pray and ask God to help you keep what you learned today afresh so you can have an example to list tonight.

Nightlight:

In what way have you chosen to "Look on Purpose" in these last couple of days (making a connection with what you read in Scripture and the world around you)?

One day while on family vacation, I was stuck inside our rented beach house with a cold. But because of the pause in my day, I was able to see something of true beauty. On this last day of our trip, my view from the house was a straight shot to the canopy where my whole family was playing. I felt like I was watching the finale of *Parenthood*. I'm sorry, I know. If you need to pause here because of your own hang-ups with NBC ratings, I get it. For the rest of you, keep reading.

Right there, everything was coming together before my eyes. It started with my grandfather, the patriarch. He passed away six years ago, and this scene in my mind started with the strong sense that he was just loving what we were up to, especially since all of our vacation antics this week included my 81-year-old grandmother. The blue Frisbee® flying through the air symbolized the seemingly effortless play between all four generations present. Sisters and cousins normally separated by busy schedules spent a week together digging in the sand. Husband and wife reunited at the stroke of midnight after commuting to work back and forth across Texas. No one knew what time it was, and cell phones remained in a bucket at the front door. Though no scene is perfect, and not everyone could be there, it really did feel like a culmination of many stories. My warm feelings heated up even more with the realization that this was not, in fact, *Parenthood*. This was not a television show. This was *my family*.

We all want the experience. We might joke about living vicariously through someone else and her status updates, but that is never our real desire. It's why the marketing directors for Walt Disney World entice us to "Experience the Magic." The catch phrase isn't "Read about the Magic" or "Look at Someone Else's Magic." No, its media casts a vision—*you could actually experience this*.

Many women share this sincere cry, "I know God's truth in my head, but I don't feel it in my heart." They want to know it with their whole being—not just in the rational part of their brain. They also want to know it with the emotional part. Although the Christian walk is certainly not lived out by feelings alone, we know the security beneath us is meant to be owned.

Even though people want and need to experience, many feel trapped. Like the promises of God were meant for others but not them. They read the precious words of God's promises and wonder if the good parts are for someone else, while they are doomed for destruction. It seems life already dealt them an unfavorable hand, and the more they talk about their pain, the more it appears confirmed. So now what?

Here's the good news. God's plan is not for some of us to walk with Him and others to be spectators.

If you're not convinced you too were invited for a full-out vibrant experience with God, let me share some current scientific findings. Brain research has confirmed our brains remain changeable throughout life. Because of this, we now know that the results of our negative feeling and thinking responses, including those stemming from our early relationships, can be reversed. Cutting edge neuroscientist Dan Siegel states, "The brain changes in response to experience."[18] For better or worse, our experiences got us where we are today, and they are our strategy for change.

This is where it gets really good. Research is now saying our relationship experiences with God use the same special part of the brain that even secular scientists agree changes the deepest parts of us making us feel "stuck" emotionally.[19] I'm still in awe over this one.

Only a Creator with healing in mind from the beginning would make us this way.

God often uses experiences with others (parents, spouses, mentors, counselors) to activate the special part of the brain I'm referencing (the attachment system). But *His* involvement in your healing process is timeless, always available, and non-circumstantial. God arranged it so our experiences with Him, the unchanging God of stability, could be an accessible part of our healing.

This sense of having a relationship with God releases a chemical in us called oxytocin.[20] If you happen to do an Internet search for oxytocin, you'll find the chemical is known to help heal wounds—physical wounds. Is that perfect or ironic? Or God's seamless paradox? We all have emotional wounds. We all need healing in some parts of our minds, the house of our memories, leading us to a wide range of reactions in life and relationships. This is just more evidence of your wonderful makeup and God's plan, laced with hope at every corner.

What does this reality mean to you?

Read Psalm 103. Journal what sticks out to you as you learn about God. Then take a step back and look at this snapshot. *This is your family.*

Specifically, look at verse 3. How many sins does He forgive?

How many diseases does He heal?

I know there are some who are struggling today with unhealed diseases. This does not mean God's Word is wrong in its declaration. One day, for the Christian, the diseases will all be healed, either in this short life or in the one that lasts forever. The focus here is that He is the one Who heals them. All of them. The ones we think of and the ones unseen. He wants to heal our emotional ones as well as our physical and spiritual ones.

Here we have our last action point in the S.A.L.E. acronym:

Experience it for Yourself

Let's list all of the actions we've learned here:

S:

A:

L:

E:

You can't experience apart from stamping (believing by faith). You'll definitely get caught on the spiritual treadmill if you forget to ask for help. And you can't go deeper without seeking. All three are involved as we participate in the element of experience, a powerful place of growth and enthusiasm. I used to think the experience portion was equivalent to the climax. But the experience part is no more important than the previous three. The crescendo is the story God writes with you at each step of the process.

Satan doesn't want us to know that there's more we can do with what God has given us. He sure doesn't want us to know we can go from surface knowledge to application. He'd love for us to merely hear the truths of God, and just let it sit like stale water. Encounters with God happen when we turn what we learn into action. The image of bubbling, living water emerges.

"My heart has heard you say, "Come and talk with me."
"And my heart responds, "Lord, I am coming."

Psalm 27:8 nlt

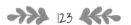

What does this verse give you a picture of?

What picture does this verse give you with regard to God wanting you to experience more than just knowing things in your head?

Week 5 Day Four

"My simple and profound observation is this: those who get a true taste of His heart fall in love. Once your appetite is stimulated, it will be hard to shake the craving. Other than your salvation, your Abba experience will be the most important experience of your entire Christian life."[21] Dave Busby

Well, enough of this. We can't talk about how important experiential activity is through dozens of paragraphs; we have to discuss how to put this into action. Let's dive in to some examples that give us a picture of how this works.

Dave Busby (quoted in Days Two and Four of this week) was a teacher of monumental influence to me in my youth, as he was the first to show me how to experience God in such a personal way. He devoted ample time discussing the problem of knowing something but not experiencing it, namely the love of a father. He wrote the following excerpt, which he labeled as one of his "Abba Daddy Experiences:"

"I encountered the Father's heart again while participating at a summer camp in Waco, Texas. During break time, I was relaxing at the hotel pool where I was staying, and I noticed two young boys playing in the water. The younger boy was decked out in the most outrageous water gear I have ever seen. Snorkels, masks, and fins seemed to protrude from every corpuscle of his body! As the boys splashed around, they muttered that their dad, who was supposed to join them earlier, had not yet arrived.

I laid on my beach chair nearly asleep when the Holy Spirit seemed to whisper, "David, wake up. Sit up. Look toward the door of the pool." As I peeled my body up from the chair, I had the beautiful experience of watching the boys' father enter the pool area at last.

As I focused on the dad's face, I saw a flash of delight that came over him as he saw his younger son dressed up in his ridiculous gear. At that moment the Holy Spirit seemed to say to me, 'The flash of delight on this dad's face as he beholds his son is simply because this boy is his. It has nothing to do with his water gear. David, every time your heavenly

Father looks at you, this <u>same</u> joy lights up His face, simply because you are His boy and sometimes your behavior and attitudes are just as ridiculous as this boy's pool garb.' I wept. Our Daddy delights in us because we are <u>His</u>."[22]

What do you feel when you read Dave's story? (There are no wrong answers here.)

The "how much more phrase" from Matthew 7:9-11 echoes. If a father on Earth treats his children this way, how much more will God creatively and boldly protect us and love us for who we are? Matthew Henry's commentary on Matthew 7:9-11 compliments this discussion: "If all the compassions of all the tender fathers in the world were crowded into the bowels of one, yet compared *with the tender mercies of our God*, they would be but as a candle to the sun, or a drop to the ocean."[23]

Dave felt the nudge from the Holy Spirit, but if this were a television show, let's imagine a timeline cue like "THREE DAYS BEFORE" written across the screen after this event at the pool. Three days before, or three weeks or years before, we would probably see Dave reading His Bible, studying about the character of God. We have to be in the Word to recognize who He is. We stamp, we ask, and then we feel the nudge from the Holy Spirit to have one of these experiences.

How do we find this to be true from a promise in John 14:26?

Like we said earlier, this is a walk. A spiritual walk. A Spirit-led walk. Not an excursion where we serve as the camp activity director. God is preaching to me right now. It's His job to remind us. Take heart, He will do that for His children.

There's a lot of talk today about living in community and the desire to "do life together" with people. The heart of God is for this to be that way with you. I write this with such passion and awe. It is His heart for you to experience.

Consider and write the loving, relational command in 1 Thessalonians 5:17:

Go back and revisit Deuteronomy 6:4-9. What do you notice?

Specifically, what does verse 6 mention? These commandments that I give to you today are to be _____ .

What is the significance of this?

You may have heard people say the phrase "walking with God" or "my walk with God." After studying this, I realize there is much more to this than perhaps our culture gives sacred credit. I hope it means more to you now, too.

I'll share one of my "Abba Daddy Experiences." It was our first Wednesday night with the "new youth guy." First Wednesday night, first any night. We'd never laid eyes on him. Change in a youth group is *just hard*. This stage is full of emotional, hormonal, needy and wonderful peeps. I remember my tears when Scot, the former youth minister, moved. He was an important leader, the one I knew since I entered the youth group in seventh grade. And now, as a sophomore, he was leaving. Funny thing, though. The first night with the new guy was actually more memorable than the tears of Scot's departure. Remember that.

I can vividly recall the room we were in, watching this man give his first lesson as he graciously sprinkled in trivia about his life we'd find interesting. I say that in all seriousness; I really did want to know about his wife, his kids, his anniversary. He told us all these things. But it's what he said after his trivia that locked the whole night up into a steel trap in my mind. It wasn't what he told us about himself; it's what he told us about *us*. Mind you, we were a nametag-less youth group.

I can't even tell this story to myself without starting to cry. As he told us about his life and hobbies and what God was teaching him, he started working us into his story. "And maybe you've felt this way before, Derek . . . " A few minutes passed. "I'm glad you made it tonight, Sarah." And, "God is for you, not against you, *Courtney*." As he said my name, he looked right at me. He'd done the same thing to the others, but it hits home when it's you. As my pastor says, "It's not valuable unless it's personal." Well, this got surprisingly personal. What in the world was going on? This was no joke. This guy was the real deal.

We found out the new minister received pictures and names of the teens in the youth group before he came. He studied them as if he were memorizing the church's mission statement, because to him, this was the mission statement. This guy was legit. He wanted to know each one of us even before he arrived. This was not to expose an impressive talent; he simply cared to know us by name the first night. He wanted to show us we were valuable to him, and the details of our lives mattered. He was already in a place of leadership to us, and he certainly did not waste the respect and title he was granted. It was the Lord reaching down and scooping up each one of us as we experienced an attribute of God that took us back by pure wonder. The parallel with how God cares about each of us was so strong. I cannot think of that night without moistened eyes of surprise and joy.

This is how God cares about you. He studies you, and not because he has to. He studies you because you are His and He wants to. His loving you is the mission statement—not religion. The Lord orchestrated the whole thing. He taught Troy, our youth minister, how to love and made this a priority in his heart because it is such a natural virtue of God's character. He looks me in the eye; He knows my name. And one day I will see it and hear it. It will be a replay of what happened that night but on a much, much grander scale.

Remember, one of the best parts is this is not solely what we wish for God to be. These are attributes that we see in Scripture. We can know these are true and accept these experiences as the weaving of the Holy Spirit in our lives.

I wonder how God allowed the Samaritan woman to experience Him after her initial visit. She probably never looked at the well or her path to it in the same way. The well, once symbolizing striving and painstaking labor, now represented a change of her soul. Even though some of her relationships with the townspeople might have improved, don't you picture her making a few more noon-day trips to the well just to re-live her personal time with her Savior? I do. Maybe this is where she sat down and rehearsed what He said, her feet making figure eights in the sand as she pondered the dialogue once again. His truth resurrected as she saw with her own two eyes the exact spot where He sat. This must have been a joy for the woman to put her faith imagination to work. With the word pictures of her testimony surrounding her, she had a physical way to experience it all over again.

We may not be able to relate to using our five senses to experience something at a water well, but we can relate to modern-day scenarios turning an experience with God into a memory. For example, many of us can identify with a time where we dreaded coming home to something on the other side of the door. Jingling keys. Deep breaths. Rehearsing what to say or what you can't say. Your mind thinking of thousands of scenarios once you enter.

* * *

"A miserable looking woman recognized F. B. Meyer on the train and ventured to share her burden with him. For years she had cared for a crippled daughter who brought great joy to her life. She made tea for her each morning, then left for work, knowing that in the evening the daughter would be there when she arrived home. But the daughter had died, and the grieving mother was alone and miserable. Home was not "home" anymore.

Meyer gave her wise counsel. "When you get home and put the key in the door," he said, "Say aloud, 'Jesus, I know You are here!' and be ready to greet Him directly when you open the door. And as you light the fire tell Him what has happened during the day; if anybody has been kind, tell Him; if anybody has been unkind, tell Him, just as you would have told your daughter. At night stretch out your hand in the darkness and say, 'Jesus, I know You are here!'"

Some months later, Meyer was back in that neighborhood and met the woman again, but he did not recognize her. Her face radiated joy instead of announcing misery. "I did as you told me," she said, "and it has made all the difference in my life, and now I feel I know Him."[24]

* * *

The once miserable woman took her faith imagination seriously. She chose to believe Jesus was already on the other side of that door, awaiting her debriefing of the day. And, in fact, He most certainly was.

Engraving Question/Journal Entry:

End today's study with a time of journaling an "Abba Daddy Experience" if you are nudged by a thought of one. If you cannot think of one, please mark this page so you can return to it and write a journal entry another day. Please re-record major thoughts in the back of the book, or vice versa—jot down notes here and write the longer entry in the back of the book. Either way, THIS IS SOMETHING to be told and retold to your heart and to others. You'll want to share this for sure.

B egin today by reading Joshua 4. I always think it's interesting to discover the Lord dried up the sea not once, but twice, in history for His children to cross dry land!

Joshua 4:19-24 gives us a wonderful charge and example of maintaining the experience and making it tangible. What was it?

Where is the exact location they were to retrieve the items? (See Joshua 4:2-3).

How many times is this specific place mentioned in Chapter 4?

Why do you think God wanted them to come from this exact spot?

Part of owning the memory is *allowing* yourself to have a moment of experience. This creates the appropriate space in our minds to be preoccupied with promise instead of life's problems. When God gives you a word and takes it from a phrase in your head to actual experience, this is something you want to remember. Memories take time to stick in our minds. As a society, we often do a poor job of securing the precious phrases.

After we have these experiences with the Lord, how can we make sure they "stick," in order to remember them well?

There are some tangible ways to make these moments gel in our minds like Joshua and the Israelites did. Enhance your memory of these times with the Lord by finding a memento that reminds you. In the story of the lonely woman, perhaps she had a rise of gladness in her heart when she saw the special key she kept beside her Bible.

My husband laughs (and cringes) when we pass a gift shop on vacation. He doesn't worry about spending money as much as he knows he'll lose me for a few hours of the trip. I do love a souvenir store. There's something about remembering by holding a momento in your hand.

Going back to the middle of the Jordan River costs you something, but it's worth it.

It will take time, it may involve extra emotions, but just because it's easier to keep walking once you've crossed the Jordan, doesn't mean it is better to do so. God knew His people would not be ultimately satisfied with a shell from the shore. They needed to go back to the middle. But we want to go on with our day sometimes. We don't think we have time. We don't want to stop and ponder and retrieve mentally or physically. We certainly don't want to run back into those grayer places and relive some emotions we've left behind. In verse 10, we see the Israelites "hurried" across the river. This was referring to the group as a whole, not necessarily the twelve men who returned, but if the people hurried, I think the men who went back might have hurried a bit with their twelve important treasures as well. Remember when you re-enter the waters, you are with God now. He isn't doing this to re-flood you. And it's ok to hurry back with Him holding your hand. We have to be wise, and certainly, I would not suggest you re-enter a dangerous situation or relationship. But going back mentally and making a memory to hold in your hand as a sign of deliverance, to remember God's power in your rescue, will be worth it.

Go back through some of the Scripture and take a minute to think about what has been meaningful to you so far in the study. What tangible items can you correlate to help you remember and cement your experience?

Would you consider collecting one of these items?

What was the purpose of the stones in Joshua 4:19-24, and who was to benefit from the story?

What does Psalm 102:18 say?

We see evidence of God working this way through the stones in Joshua 4. We also see Jesus using these tools of the tangible as He spoke in parables throughout His ministry. When He did this, He wanted the disciples and those who had soft hearts to His Word to have understanding from their prior experiences. He also wanted them to be able to see these objects again in the future and link them back to His teachings.

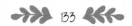

Choose ONE of the following parables and stories of Jesus and see how this method of remembering via the tangible could be true for you, as well as those under His teaching at the time:

Parable of the Mustard Seed (Matthew 13:31-32)

Parable of the Yeast (Matthew 13:33)

Parable of the Sheep (Matthew 18:12-14)

Parable of the Lost Coin (Luke 15:8-10)

Parable of the Fishing Net (Matthew 13:47-50)

The First Lord's Supper (Luke 22:14-19, **perhaps the most important object lesson***)*

The Holy Spirit will gently guide you and inspire you with what you can have as an object for remembering. Obviously, you can't do this with every moment with the Lord. There are other ways of helping to experience and recall His faithfulness. Not only is sharing a beneficial way to help us remember, it also helps others greatly. Writing is also a powerful memory tool; it "sets" the floating ideas in our brain as a future souvenir of God's faithfulness. These two combined make so much sense in the command in Psalm 102:18. But as much as it makes sense, the effects of the written praise are beyond our comprehension. We have no idea what God could do with it in the years to come.

And again, we trust our Wonderful Counselor (Isaiah 9:6) with the rest of our remembering for the journey. Take a look at what the disciple John wrote at the end of his book. What does the last verse of the book of John say? (John 21:25)

Amazing. That's our God.

The joy that we have to live in the unveiled reality of God's promises is so sacred, it cannot be boiled down to the tangible alone. My heart is beating faster just thinking about this. It's so simple and yet so profound all at once. It says in Matthew 13:34-35:

> *"Jesus told the crowds all these things in parables, and He would not speak anything to them without a parable, so that what was spoken through the prophet might be fulfilled:*
>
> *'I will open My mouth in parables;*
> *I will declare things kept secret*
> *from the foundation of the world.' "*

Since the creation of the world, these were kept disclosed. Now these things are revealed for us to live, and live on. For right now.

Week 6

End with
a Twirl

Week 6 · Day One

"What a God we have! And how fortunate we are to have him, this Father of our Master Jesus! Because Jesus was raised from the dead, we've been given a brand-new life and have everything to live for, including a future in heaven—and the future starts now! God is keeping careful watch over us and the future. The Day is coming when you'll have it all—life healed and whole."

1 PETER 1:3-5 MSG

Hair color. Hometown. Favorite movie. When I started dating Josh, my parents wanted to know every detail about this guy. Mom reacted the most when I rattled off his birthday. Growing up in the much safer, you-can-play-outside-with-the-neighbors era, my mom has some neat childhood memories. Some of the favorites my sister and I have heard many times include hopscotch, riding bikes, playing with the family of seven kids, and last but definitely not least—Susie Cunningham. As the story goes, my mom remember her as the girl who happily bounded out of her house to play. If anyone asked, "When is your birthday?" she would always have the same spunky response, "December 18th . . . Here comes Christmas!" Susie must have had some pretty responsive parents who made sure their daughter knew she was special and perhaps handpicked to herald the pep rally exactly one week before the big day. The memory of Susie's response still makes my mom laugh, so when I married someone whose birthday was December 18, Mom thought she won the jackpot.

I inherited some of this December drama. As a child, one of my favorite holiday memories occurred when my mom hung the red felt rectangle on the hallway door of our home. I can still feel the dark wood paneling that served as the backdrop to this ever-important decoration, the advent calendar. Symmetric boxes outlined twenty-five days of anticipation leading up to Christmas morning.

I was a preteen when I decided my favorite day of the year was December 23rd. Yes, Christmas Eve is a blast, but how much more exciting to have the whole 24 hours BEFORE Christmas Eve still on deck. In our family, there's not anything particular happening on the 23rd—no early Christmas celebrations—no special traditions lending that day more prominence. It's simply the fact of knowing it's all up ahead. The forty-eight hours before Christmas excite me because of two words: *untainted anticipation.* For a moment, we can know the best parts have not even touched us yet.

The days preceding Christmas are attractive to me because of the sandwich of promise they deliver. On one side, there's what we look forward to in a couple of days. But there must be something of worth about the 23rd itself, otherwise Christmas Day would be the pick. Not only is something ahead, the spirit in the air is current. Holiday mode is in full swing.

In the same way, we can experience what I call the "residual glitter of Heaven," as we live aware of what we have going for us both today and in the future of eternity. We can take a minute and dwell on what we are going to experience as well as the current Spirit we have with us. These are things to be excited about right now. You and I have an opportunity to abide in anticipation like a child in the forty-eight hours preceding Christmas morning.

Sadly, I believe you and I are living in a December 23rd world, but operating like it's December 26th. Like it's all over. Like the best parts of our lives have passed. Like all the fun that's left is just for the kids, and our destiny is to help clean up the kitchen.

What about you? According to this analogy, do you think you live like it's December 23rd or 26th ? Explain your thoughts.

What do the following verses say about what we have to look forward to?

Malachi 4:2

1 Corinthians 13:12

Revelation 21:1-5

Let's look again at 1 Peter 1:3-5 from today's lesson. What is God's encouraging promise?

What if we as women adopted the truth that we can live every day like it's December 23ʳᵈ? We could live this way if we believe all we have built up in our hearts and that all the excitement is not waning with age but is still yet to come. All of these truths we learn about in the Bible and at church are actually what we have to look forward to every day. We have the chance to realize the spiritual excitement opportunities surrounding us now. Our past, which God lovingly knows. Our present, in which we enjoy His companionship. Our future, where we look forward to heaven. This is our different way to daydream.

Remember our discussion in Week One about the "Song of Anticipation?" We said a great place in the Bible to insert a holy song of anticipation would be just seconds before Jesus reveals Himself to the Samaritan woman.

"The woman said, 'I know that Messiah" (called Christ) is coming. When he comes, he will explain everything to us' " (John 4:25, NIV). [the background music hits an all-time high]

"Then Jesus declared, 'I, the one speaking to you—I am he." (v. 26).

You know the feeling you have when you are in a new relationship, and you can smile for seemingly no reason? You're happy just knowing in the back of your mind you have the relationship brewing? This is how we can feel when we recall we are in an alive, personal relationship as described in the peak of this true story. What would it do to remind you that you are like the Samaritan woman in these verses?

What would your life look like if you were constantly dwelling on the fact that you are in the middle of a dynamic love relationship?

As a young teen, one night we went house hunting as a family. While normally this activity would have equated to absolute boredom to a 13-year-old, this time it didn't, and the Lord allowed me to remember it vividly. I looked out over the stranger's backyard, and my mind drifted to the events of the day at school. I just struck up a friendship with the "new kid." The boredom usually accompanying such a trip took a backseat. It didn't matter where I was or what I was doing; I was happy because my mind was preoccupied with thoughts of my new friend.

The only way for our preoccupation with promise to win in our minds is to keep it in our active, short-term memory.

What is something that brings you joy to be reminded of in a present-tense situation? No homework when you (or your children) are out of school? That diapers are miles away when you are on a date with your husband? What is it for you?

This active, short term memory can work for us or against us. Think about it in the situation of a social gathering. What our mind dwells on can either cause confidence and peace or insecurity whirled with anxiety. At the heart of it all, whether you are all alone or in a group (but especially in a group setting), the following is true: **You want to have something to say**. When the questions come like, "So, what do you do?" "Do you have kids?" "What do you do for fun?"—it's deemed acceptable to have something to say.

But let's face it, whether we actually voice it or not really isn't the issue. It's about *knowing* and *feeling* we have something great going on in our lives—something filling. We all know people who have great degrees and promotions to flaunt but live with empty emotional tanks. The thing "going on" in your life right now as a believer in Christ brings joyful humility—the awareness of how much companionship you have with Christ.

Not because of anything you did, but because of Who He is, you can celebrate that you also are a girl who has someone. And this is not just any someone. When you consider this Someone is a person Who gave His life for you, it adds an entirely different dimension to what we are talking about. The times I am consciously thinking about this fact, I walk into a room with confidence and a true, unshakable smile. I just want you to know this: you've got something majorly exciting going on right now in case you were not aware.

How often has the "thing" in the back of our minds been the latest relationship concern, a present burden, or our to-do list?

Look up the psalmist's declaration in Psalm 63:6.

Oh, what our lives would be and our hearts would look like if we were at this spot! What do you currently think of if you wake up at night? What would you like your mind to think on?

This is us being preoccupied with promise instead of life's problems.

I picture this process much like the kneading of dough in a person's mind. Those in the Bible who declared this affinity for dwelling on God made a conscious decision to let the promise of God's presence roll over and over and over in their minds. Going from:

Discipline   Refreshing habit

Pleasant activity

I have a passionate vision that this could be the new tape running through our heads that no one can take away (see Romans 8:38-39). That these truths we are learning serve as the thing in the back of our minds at all times—not as a legalistic rule—but an easily accessible memory for sure-fire joy.

gain, maybe your Christmas experiences were more disenchanting than delightful, so it's hard to relate to this December 23rd example. Maybe two days before Christmas reminds you more of dreading Christmas because Aunt Tina always complains about your cooking, the kids have the croup, not a single gift has been wrapped, and what you'd really like to do is lock yourself in a room with John Grisham's grand idea and skip Christmas. We've all had those types of days, too. But in reality, you too can choose to live like it's all in store for you, like the days leading up to Christmas we all dream of.

At the time I began this week's introduction (the story about my mom's childhood neighbor and holiday anticipation), I was also reading through the Old Testament books of the Bible in my personal time of study. Particularly, the timing coincided with reading of the brief, two-chapter book of Haggai.

Dive in to Haggai 1:1-10 and get the scoop on how this story begins.

What would you say is the summary of what the Lord of Heaven's Armies said to Haggai? What were the people supposed to do? What had they been doing?

Continue with verses 12-14. When Haggai relayed God's message to the people, what was their response?

What four words in verse 13 served as a literal game changer?

What did those four words do to the people, according to verse 14?

The Bible says this "stirred up the Spirit" of the governor, the high priest and "OF ALL THE REMNANT OF THE PEOPLE" (Haggai 1:14, [emphasis mine]). With one statement, the people were on board, reinvigorated to complete their calling. Out of heart, not out of duty. God's presence brought an entirely new perspective. The New Living Translation tells us this announcement "sparked the enthusiasm" of every one of God's people. I love the wording here! The result of this knowledge led to a wave of vibrancy. Unprompted by man and therefore sustained by God. The black and white screen just went total Technicolor®.

Let's continue in chapter 2 of Haggai, but only through verse 9. Then we have to talk.

Since I was specifically reading Haggai literally right after I wrote the opener for this section, just imagine how my jaw dropped when I came to the book's conclusion in Haggai 2:18. At the time, for that day, the Lord had me reading out of the New Living Translation. He knew why. If you do not have an NLT version of the Bible, and do not have access to look it up online, do not fear. I have it listed for you at the bottom of today's lesson. HOWEVER, if you do have your own copy or a way to read verses 9-19 right now in the New Living Translation, do it! I'm so excited not only to show you what God showed me, but I'm even more thrilled you get to make the discovery. Ok, I'll calm down and get back to it.

What did you discover?

(If you do not have the NLT, flip to the back of today's lesson now to find the text). I mean, really—jaw drop.

The footnote in the NLT tells us several of the dates (from the Hebrew lunar calendar) mentioned in Haggai accurately correspond to our modern calendar based on surviving Persian records. I felt it was NO COINCIDENCE the Lord primed my heart with the message to live like it's all still ahead, and then I read this charge to dwell on December 18th, because the Lord has a promise for us!

Three times in the final sections of this book, we find mention of the special day of remembrance on December 18th. In the beginning of Haggai 2, the Lord compared the former glorious temple of Solomon, to the current temple they were working on, and finally to the incomparable temple that was to come.

In verse 9, the Lord says He "will provide peace in this place." It is cross-referenced in the *Holman Christian Standard Bible* to Isaiah 9:6. Look up what this verses says. How neat is *that*?

December 18th, here comes Christmas; December 18th; here comes Christ.

God commanded the people and He's calling us to do the same: Think carefully. Ponder intentionally. He's saying, "Keep what I've told you alive. Stir it up so it stirs you up. Think about this. Remember."

For the people in the book of Haggai, December 18th marked God's gracious promise to forgive the past and promised continued blessing for the people's obedience.

Look again at what Haggai 2:19 says:

He said to them, "I am giving you a promise now while the seed is still in the barn. You have not yet harvested your grain, and your grapevines, fig trees, pomegranates, and olive trees have not yet produced their crops. But from this day onward I will bless you" (NLT).

God is telling us the very same thing. Through His mercy, He is giving these delightful truths of His love, protection, companionship, adoration, and intimacy. And yet, the hope of these "crops" may still look like seeds.

How does this promise from Haggai (2:19) encourage us as we journey through taking God's promises from head knowledge to heart knowledge?

What promise from God's Word can you apply to the "pomegranate seed" in your life as you consider Haggai 2:19? This serves as your Engraving Question. You may expand your answer in the back of the book.

Who else in your life needs to be encouraged with this hope?

While our seed is still in the barn, He's promising us the very same thing He told the people in the book of Haggai. We have a sustaining promise in this tumultuous life. *He is with us.* He is with *you.* In this current moment, He wants us to apply this knowledge to our hearts though the tiniest seed hasn't left the feed sack. This can encourage us when we feel so far from feeling alive in a relationship with Christ. It may seem far off to you. You may still feel as if your insides are more stale than bubbling. That's the beauty of His giving us a promise now, even though the seed is still in the barn. His promise is valid and fully claimable—no matter how you feel or physically see right this moment.

He wants you and me to live like it's harvest time. He is telling us to go ahead and believe in His fatherhood to you. In His desire and ability to know you. To go ahead and enjoy this relationship. For everything you can imagine is through His Word. And then some. God would not have made such a big deal about family, either with His own Father/Son relationship with Jesus or our place as His children, if it weren't true.

What does Jesus say to you in John 14:2?

He addresses this promise of our place in His home in John 14 and then specifically adds His confirmation to us. He knows we need to hear it again and in a different way sometimes. He knows us so well.

This is why we can go ahead and embrace this pre-Christmas spirit, or "the residual glitter of Heaven." Jesus has taught us a thing or two here about Christmas and barnyard bliss. I'm specifically addressing the December 23rd we all desire—the one where you know in two days you have a place where you belong. There's a front door with a wreath and jingle bells where someone is expecting you. There will be a spot just for you at a certain table. You'll bring something to contribute. You anticipate laughter, stories, and a happy belly. There's a spirit of peace, and celebration is fitting.

These things are true. Someone is expecting you. There's a place at His table where His banner over you shouts love. Warmth awaits. Hugs aren't hurried or obligatory. This is the moment we all wait for. Can you see how this spirit of excitement spills over into the present if we believe this is *exactly* what's in store for us?

Haggai 2:9-19 NLT

> *"The future glory of this Temple will be greater than its past glory, says the Lord of Heaven's Armies. And in this place I will bring peace. I, the Lord of Heaven's Armies, have spoken!"*

On December 18 of the second year of King Darius's reign, the Lord sent this message to the prophet Haggai: "This is what the Lord of Heaven's Armies says. Ask the priests this question about the law: 'If one of you is carrying some meat from a holy sacrifice in his robes and his robe happens to brush against some bread or stew, wine or olive oil, or any other kind of food, will it also become holy?'"

The priests replied, "No."

Then Haggai asked, "If someone becomes ceremonially unclean by touching a dead person and then touches any of these foods, will the food be defiled?"

And the priests answered, "Yes."

Then Haggai responded, "That is how it is with this people and this nation, says the Lord. Everything they do and everything they offer is defiled by their sin. Look at what was happening to you before you began to lay the foundation of the Lord's Temple. When you hoped for a twenty-bushel crop, you harvested only ten. When you expected to draw fifty gallons from the winepress, you found only twenty. I sent blight and mildew and hail to destroy everything you worked so hard to produce. Even so, you refused to return to me, says the Lord.

"Think about this eighteenth day of December, the day when the foundation of the Lord's Temple was laid. Think carefully."

I am giving you a promise now while the seed is still in the barn. You have not yet harvested your grain, and your grapevines, fig trees, pomegranates, and olive trees have not yet produced their crops. But from this day onward I will bless you."

Nightlight:

Reflect what you wrote about your own "pomegranate seed" in life (from page 147).

Week 6 Day Three

Remember my grandmother, Jajo? Well, she had a BFF. You can only imagine this duo. No kidding, her name was Flo, and everyone in town knew "Flo." One of the things she would always say reminds me of today's challenge, as well as Psalm 90:12. Flo's mantra was "Life is not a dress rehearsal." So, ladies, let's do this, let's learn this, thorough and well.

We're going to have a challenge today. When I say the word *challenge*, let's not be avoidant; rather, be uplifted. In a parent-child relationship, appropriate challenge is a gentle championing for a new success with the help of the parent. We can be confident of that help.

In the middle of our last week together, this day will serve as a necessary review day. Sometimes we just need extra time to squeeze out all God intends for us. It's one of those things where you "get out of it what you put in." So if we're all in, let's really get this down and make these habits. It typically takes 30 days for something to become a habit. In this case with changing our thoughts, I would say it takes at least that. As my kids' swim instructor says, "Hard things become easy when you practice them." That's where we are. Are you in?

On Week Four: Day Two, we worked on the template of our thoughts and feelings. Return to that page and read what you wrote. Because we are human, sometimes when we first try something, we choose an easy topic (I do this too, so no judgment). If you happened to choose an easy example, I challenge you to choose an additional example and go a little deeper.

Emotion:

Situation:

Possible Thought Chain:

Specific Thought Summary (brief, bullet points):

Replacement Thoughts (using truth from Scripture):

A sincere "Good work" to you. I'm proud of you and you can KNOW that God is.

Let's go back to Week Four: Day Three where we interacted with our friends, S, M, and A. Return to the section where we filled in the blanks. Read what you filled in:

If I am _____ ,

God is able to _____ .

but even if He does not, _____ .

Consider how you have grown since then. How have you applied this lesson in your life? Take some time on this.

What is an additional example you can learn today for an additional tool to renew your mind?

1. *If we are/I am* _____ *("thrown into the blazing furnace", v. 17).*

2. *God is able to* _____

3. *But even if He does not,* _____ *(your action)*

How are you doing with regards to Satan's attempts to interfere? Are you getting held up on any specific area? (See Week Two: Days Two, Three, and Four).

Recall the story about my Hunter saying, "Mommy Get Choo." What name of God will you call on today? (See Week Four: Day Two).

In addition to the name you listed, in light of any of these questions you may be struggling with, or anything else the Enemy is throwing at you, call on The Favorite Shield, Jesus today.

One of the verses we memorized as a family last year was Psalm 8:2,

> *"Through the praise of children and infants*
> *you have established a stronghold against your enemies,*
> *to silence the foe and the avenger." (NIV)*

Nancy Guthrie writes in her devotional book that God says, "I will lift you out of your hopelessness, moving you from the desperation of the pit to the security of a rock. And when I do, you will sing. All of the old songs will be new." [25]

Sing on, like a child of God, because you are one. Sing away; put the Enemy on mute. Sing because of what you now know . . . really, really know.

Week 6 Day Four

"Mommy, what's wrong with that lady's dress? It doesn't twirl . . ."
(said a young girl to her mother)

Begin today by reading Psalm 91 in preparation for God to speak to your heart.

I'm going to do a little storytelling today . . .

Since my second child was a girl, "they" said she would surely imitate my baby days, and be my never-ending burst of energy—a.k.a. my non-sleeper. While Paisley was in my tummy, I secretly prayed for God to prove them all wrong. I learned that when God answers a prayer, He doesn't hold back.

Granted, we had our moments, and our days, but overall, Paisley was my put-the-lounge-chair-on-the-lowest-rung-and-*bask*-baby. Since she was super chill and loved her sleep, I naively thought once we got past the tortuous tummy time phase, Paisley and I would coast, not having any huge obstacles until we tried to do algebra together.

At her six-month check-up, we found out differently. Everything checked out fine until the doctor took a final look at Paisley's forehead. The doctor frowned and said he was concerned. After referring us to a surgeon for follow-up, I asked him what his worst case scenario might be. He stared silently straight ahead. Finally, he acknowledged me. "I'd like you to call the specialist, and get his opinion."

Surgeons confirmed a diagnosis of craniosynostosis, a rare condition in which one or more of the sutures in a baby's skull is fused together prematurely. This caused misshape of her forehead, which would worsen over time. The optimal treatment window for us was when Paisley turned 11 months old. This translated into five long months of what ifs, preparation, prayer, and plenty of "are you still awakes?" lobbed across our king-sized-bed in the middle of the night.

My primary concerns were psychological, not physical or neurological. Typical mom-doubts of when to start sleep training and crying it out were intensified. What if she doesn't know how to go to a stranger? What if she feels abandoned? What about the part where I cannot be with her? What if she doesn't know how to fall asleep? I worked for years with families and children on bonding and attachment. I felt like I knew too much to be comforted. And yet, one colleague responded to the news about the surgery with, "You know what to do in this situation."

I did?

You can totally hear my confidence, no?

Months later, God gave me a specific word. I felt Him tell me there would not be *one second* she would be alone. It sounds funny, but I thought many times about how God would be with her, yet it did not calm me as much as when it was worded to me this way. To know she would never be alone, not even for a second, was the wording my heart needed to hear. This gave an answer to my many questions and single over-arching fear.

God prepped our hearts in those lingering months over and over again. By the time we reached that pivotal date on the calendar, we actually felt peace. Peace mixed in with that gut punch of a nightmare feeling, but still more peace than dread.

The morning of her procedure, Paisley drank some "goofy juice," making her relaxed for her trip to the operating room. Then it was time. Seventeen pounds wrapped in a thin tiger hospital gown bounced down the hall with a nurse we knew for all of three minutes.

Hours earlier than expected, the nurse not only answered our unspoken concerns of survival, but said our baby came through it perfectly. It was only a matter of minutes until we could join Paisley in her room. It still baffles me all the pieces God orchestrated (and that's speaking of the parts we knew about). I think our smiles literally floated us up to the ICU waiting room.

But personally, one of the hardest parts on this mommy awaited. The surgeon called us back to see her. It's hard for me to see anyone lying lethargic in a hospital bed, but I'm convinced lying littles are the worst.

For the next 36 hours, we watched the expected, yet wearisome side effects begin to come over her body. Her eyelids turned a bruised, bright plum purple, her fever spiked and—the worst—the intense head swelling caused her eyes to shut. *For several days.* As relaxed of a baby as Paisley was, she was also known for a spunkiness in her eyes that was never meant to disappear.

Throughout the journey leading up to the surgery and post-operation, the Strong family seed was definitely still in the barn. Yes, we held enormous gratitude for making it through the surgery, but we were in rough times. In the last week of June while other families were at their neighborhood swimming pools and playing evening Putt-Putt, Josh and I celebrated 9 years of marriage with a cupcake from the hospital lobby. Fuchsia icing drizzled a tired "Happy Anniversary" on top. We were back on newborn hours of sleep. Paisley's bruising, lethargy, and fevered body mixed with our own sleep deprivation almost made us wonder why we did this in the first place.

I rode in the back seat on the way home—holding her hand, singing to her—trying any way I could to reassure her. To think after everything she'd been through and now she couldn't see her surroundings was almost unbearable.

This was so hard on my heart until God nudged me to pray two specific prayers for her in that backseat while her eyes were shut. I began to see this as an opportunity. I asked God to show her beautiful things about Himself that she wouldn't otherwise see when she has the distractions of the world around her. I also prayed that the Lord would fulfill the promises from Psalm 91, the chapter He spoke over me as a theme when this entire journey began. Verse four says, "He will cover you with His feathers; you will take refuge under His wings. His faithfulness will be a protective shield." These verses I journaled so many months ago came alive. Covered. She now had a literal covering. And if someone has to be covered, it doesn't get much more delightful than to be covered with feathers. Think about it—what happens when a person is covered with an uncontrollable amount of something so unbelievably enchanting? Balloons. Rose petals. Waterfalls. Their eyes automatically close in the bliss of it. I prayed for that kind of covering for Paisley. That if she had to be covered, it could be this way. Where she was so preoccupied with what God showed her she would barely notice her suffering. The kind where the close is an instinctive response, with the ripple effect of a giggle and a simultaneous twirl.

Arms outstretched. Fingers free. Chin up.

Happy heart.

I have no clue what the Lord showed her mind in those days. But I really do believe the images were nothing short of engaging and beautiful. This wasn't just a fanciful thought to keep my mind off reality. Remember, the vision came from a belief that God would fulfill the promise He already spoke, "He will cover you with feathers." That's how I knew it to be true. God cut through my lack of faith and gave me enough heart to have vision for my daughter when she had none. Through my tears, I had vision for those buckets of joy-filled images to distract her from her pain. I had vision for her place of sorrow to be a playground for God to show off.

But to move her to a place of seeing anything of beauty, she had to be calmed. After weeks of strangers taking her blood and giving her shots, I can only imagine the anxiety surges she fought while she could not see.

Just like the people in the book of Haggai, the spark, the enthusiasm, the joy—had to start with the announcement of presence. "I am with you," God said.

For awhile Paisley showed the fear and frustration, but eventually she gave into restfulness, even when her body was awake. Since it is biologically impossible for the human body to be simultaneously calm and anxious, I knew she came to trust we were there. All was well.

Indeed, God answers prayers and blows the top off. He said there wouldn't be one second she would be alone. He doesn't do voids. He stuffs them full.

The people of Haggai received the promise of presence, but that was not all. God said He would *bless* them. In this case, He pointed to their barren vegetation and promised to reverse the effects of sin.

At the heart of it as parents, we are nothing if not distractors. Distractors for getting tots to open their mouths to eat. Distractors with nurture when there is hurt. Distractors with toys when they get shots. God is no different.

We distract in an effort to protect, but protection is often thought of in terms of life and death, sickness and health.

What does Psalm 5:11b-12 say God gives us on top of protection?

God wanted to bless her beyond a normal protection. And that's where we are. He is flooding us. Not only with a swift breeze as He sweeps us into rescue. But we are covered with His mighty arm *and* His feathers. The mental feathers of faith imagination we use to

see His words come uniquely alive in your everyday life this side of heaven. These are the feathers that cover to protect and literally reverse the words we or others have spoken over us—*the effects of sin.*

Paisley could not run from her covering, and neither can we. We are always destined to be covered with something.

Which will you choose to be covered with?

Covered with shame

Covered with the shadow of His hand (Isaiah 51:16)

Covered with regret

Covered with the anticipation of truth (2 Corinthians 1:20)

Covered with unforgiveness

Covered with His feathers (Psalm 91:4)

Covered with forgiveness (1 John 1:9)

As you think back to the beginning of the story, do you realize God promising "I am with you," also means "there is not one second you will be alone?" How is this good news to you?

In what situation of your life could these words be powerfully inserted? How does it change the way you feel about it? Be as specific as possible.

Who knows? Consistent with His character, Jesus could have easily ended his conversation with the woman at the well and said, "Until we meet again, girl . . . *Twirl*."

Nightlight:

Ponder the promise of Psalm 91:4 again: "He will cover you with His feathers; you will take refuge under His wings. His faithfulness will be a protective shield." Will you consciously choose to think differently next time you are in a difficult, blinding situation? What about on a normal day when everything is going ok? Beyond thinking differently, I challenge you to even take a different posture, per the title of this week's study. ☺ Journal any thoughts you have below:

And then close your eyes . . .

Fast forward three years. I am literally days from hitting the send button on this study to the publisher. The night before Paisley's first day of school—ever, she came down with something that presented as a normal stomach bug, only it continued and continued for days. She got weaker instead of better. After the emergency room trip, tests and hospital stay, she remained lethargic and unable to eat. The life was simply zapped from her, and my resident Pollyanna was losing hope.

The tired little one faced restless nights due to abdominal pain. Josh and I pulled a twin mattress beside her and took turns rubbing her stomach throughout the night. In the height of her illness, one particular night she slept much longer than normal without pain. When she woke up for the morning, even though she was still in the midst of this terrible illness, she said in a sweet four-year-old voice, "What a wonderful night!" Because she said it in almost a weak whisper, I asked her what she said. I couldn't quite understand. "What a *wonderful* night!" She dramatically said again.

The day that followed was more of the same; her eyes closed in weariness from the pain level. I had been praying Psalm 91 over her again, and I recalled this story of "The Twirl." *I should be praying again for God to show her miraculous things again of Himself while her eyes are closed.* Then I also recalled something else—the events of the night before.

Wait a minute. God knows what we need before we ask, amen? That's when I remembered her morning declaration.

He'd already done it.

And this time, she could verbalize the miracle for me.

If the woman at the well's story ended at Jesus' great reveal, it would still be an awesome account.

But the story didn't stop there. She couldn't contain it either.

What have you been excited to share in your Christian life?

After Jesus told the woman He was the Messiah she longed for, she got up. This is when she left her water jar. She returned to the town, inviting others to meet Him. The work Jesus did in her heart and mind was stronger than her lack of popularity. The Bible says *many* followed her back to the well. More importantly, once they followed, they believed.

Developing an enthusiastic heart and mind for Christ is different from other "self helps" because with most self-helps, only one self is helped. If you pick up a book from the "Dummies" series—*Cooking for Dummies, Web Hosting for Dummies, Baseball for Dummies*, you are likely reading the book for yourself. You are also likely to read this to increase your knowledge base of a particular topic while blinding others from the fact you had to use the yellow and black book to do so. There's no problem with that, but it is what it is.

Throughout the book, we've talked about God's desire to connect with *you*. Individually. Personally. In John chapter 10, Jesus describes Himself as the Good Shepherd. He further provides us with a story in describing the natural tendency of any good sheep owner, much less the perfect Creator.

"See that you don't look down on one of these little ones, because I tell you that in heaven their angels continually view the face of My Father in heaven. For the Son of Man has come to save the lost. What do you think? If a man has 100 sheep, and one of them goes astray, won't he leave the 99 on the hillside and go and search for the stray? And if he finds it, I assure you: He rejoices over that sheep more than over the 99 that did not go astray. In the same way, it is not the will of your Father in heaven that one of these little ones perish" (Matthew 18:10-14).

So believe me when I say he would have done it just for you. He would have died just for you. He loves you that much. One broken heart touched, and the Good Shepherd is overjoyed. He cared about the woman as an individual, and He was pleased to show her the good news. He would have spent the day with the Samaritan woman even if she was the only one who believed. But as it just so happened, a domino effect followed.

Developmental psychology teaches us the cure for sibling rivalry is to make sure every child knows he or she is individually cherished by the parents. Likewise, this is the very treatment the Samaritan woman received from Jesus and the catalyst that made her drop her water jug to share this love with the rest of the town. She must have felt this love so solidly from the Savior that she didn't have to hold it all to herself for fear she'd lose it. This is part of what Christ meant when He said in Him we have freedom. We are free to love others and free to share because not one ounce is taken from us when we do. It's only natural to want the Spirit to catch on once you have experienced it for yourself.

What truth discussed here or promise from Matthew 18 speaks to you?

How is this a cure for the paralyzing comparison game we often fall prey to?

Have you ever noticed after Jesus washes the disciples feet in John 13, He doesn't just tell them to love, He shows them? This time He gave an example, and He wanted the disciples to specifically love like He had loved them. After experiencing this intimate encounter with Jesus, the perspective from which they were going to love from then on was brand new.

So although the majority of the book talks about how we can help ourselves to be more aware of Christ and the personal emotional benefits from doing so, engaging in this process naturally ministers to others. We become so secure in a relationship with Him that we have nothing to lose and lots of fun to gain by spreading the enthusiasm.

Insert your pen or bookmark on this page. Look through your workbook. Ask God to bring someone to mind who could specifically benefit from something He taught you. I hope the Lord brings a specific situation of theirs you can match with a promise they need to hear today. Write their name and what you want to share with them below.

Let's revisit the topic of oxytocin, the natural chemical we discussed on Week Five: Day Three (p. 121). Known as the "cuddle hormone," oxytocin is released in our brains when we ponder our secure relationship with God. I went to a conference where this issue was addressed. Conference attendees were asked to look at a slideshow presentation of various headshots. One by one, we saw pictures of faces, but tape carefully covered up all of the facial expressions except for the eyes. We were asked to guess the emotion the person was exhibiting based on the eyes alone. At the end of the exercise, the presenter shared that the people who have the chemical oxytocin released in their brain actually do better on the test.[26] This fascinated me on a couple of levels. For one, I was still breastfeeding my son, and I noted I actually guessed some of the eye expressions the presenter labeled afterward as most difficult to determine. Breastfeeding naturally releases oxytocin. Then I began to contemplate the effect of this on human relationships in general. Could it be that as we have oxytocin from our awareness of God's presence, we are more in tune with the needs of others? Absolutely.

I've often been humbled when I recognize self-absorption and consequently, how I have "forgotten" or "not noticed" the needs of others right in front of me. Regret and repentance follow; it hurts when I realize this. But the cause and effect are obvious. "If we only knew" the love and connection we have with the Father, we would be more free to notice the needs of others because we are already filled. We too could leave behind our water jug of previous insecurities and selfishness.

Draw a water jug below. List inside the social problems you would leave behind "if you only knew . . ."

What did the woman at the well exchange them for? (refer to John 4 if needed).

What will *you* exchange the problems above for? Draw a new jug.

I bet the Master planner of this woman's life did not let ANYONE touch that water jug while she ran into town. And while He was at it, I bet He filled it with something entirely new. Although it was still physical water, the next drink—an entirely new experience.

We began this study by discussing the lesson, "If my mind can be preoccupied with problems, my mind can be preoccupied with promise." This preoccupation—being positively caught up in the promises of God—is the best form of distraction. May our minds go beyond what we've previously conceived. And we'll still be underachievers compared to what is coming.

Read Job 26:14 and write it out here:

"Everything that goes into a life of pleasing God has been miraculously given to us by getting to know, personally and intimately, the One who invited us to God. The best invitation we ever received! We were also given absolutely terrific promises to pass on to you—your tickets to participation in the life of God after you turned your back on a world corrupted by lust.

So don't lose a minute in building on what you've been given, complementing your basic faith with good character, spiritual understanding, alert discipline, passionate patience, reverent wonder, warm friendliness, and generous love, each dimension fitting into and developing the others. With these qualities active and growing in your lives, no grass will grow under your feet, no day will pass without its reward as you mature in your experience of our Master Jesus. Without these qualities you can't see what's right before you, oblivious that your old sinful life has been wiped off the books."

2 PETER 1:3-7 MSG

Conclusion

Do you remember at the beginning of our time together when I told you I'd love to be with you when you find out the truth your heart has been longing to hear? I wanted to sit across from you at your coffee table and see the pleasant relief on your face, as if you had opened an awaited present? Yes, I wish I could have witnessed these precious moments right along with you as they occurred these last six weeks. I'm confident that He who began a good work faithfully continues to complete it (Philippians 1:6). Let's point out, He's definitely not done. So, I'd also like to be there as these moments continue to pour out between you and the Lord. ENJOY!

Keep stamping, keep asking, keep looking, keep experiencing. It's going to be spectacular.

Of course, if you desire, you are ALWAYS welcome to share with me, even if I can't be at your breakfast table! Saying I'd love to hear from you would be an understatement.

email: courtney@preoccupiedwithpromise.com
website: courtneyjstrong.com

Acknowledgements

To my Savior, my God, my Father—You have cupped my face in your loving hands, so I intentionally set my gaze on You in return. Knowing You rivals (and conquers) any other affection I've ever known.

To my husband, Josh, my One and Only—Randall House didn't give me enough pages to write the tribute you deserve here. For the belief you've had in my ministry before we were even married, for your love for this message and your desire to see it lived in me, for all of the dinners you cooked AND cleaned up knowing that I only had time to literally sit down and put food in my mouth only to return to my desk to write, for all of the times you whisked me away from the computer because you knew I needed a break, for the year you gave me a Bible commentary and a domain name instead of roses, for the ways you balance out serious stuff like that with a subsequent gift of LED glowing gloves from Shark Tank, for all the ways you knew what I needed before I asked, for all of the years you supported my school, my counseling hours and practice, and endless support (in both technology and love), I just can't thank you enough. For the way you let the Spirit live out this message in you, I thank you, and I'm in love with you.

To Hunter and Paisley—The Lord has used you in so many ways to teach your daddy and me how to be preoccupied with promise. Hunter, thank you for advising me to include the word "discover" on the back jacket.

To the Original Home Group (My Dad, Mom and Sister)—You've endlessly stood by me and cheered me on. Mom and Dad, you've taught me the unconditional, surprising love of God. Dad, you told me years ago to journal what God was teaching me and that one day I could use it for something important. You constantly dream and have vision for the future, and it never ceases to inspire me. Mom, your steadfast enthusiasm, faith, and love for the Lord built a home for us as described in Proverbs 24:4. Kayla, I love you, my friend and sister. You love others and minister in ways that leave me speechless.

To My Mamps—Thank you for being one of my best friends and a spiritual leader in our family. Your life exclaims to others to "Taste and see that the Lord is good" Psalm 34:8.

To Jane, Sam, David, Avery and Abby—You guys love hard, and your consistent support has taught me so much and strengthened my heart.

To Michelle Orr with Randall House—Thank you for believing in me and in the study. You not only offered sound advice, wisdom, and encouragement, but you stayed the course with me. You desire alongside me for women to catch the hope offered within these pages.

To the editors, designers and publishing board of Randall House—Thank you for your wisdom and dedication to this project. Thank you for your help in bringing this final product to a point of sweet offering to the Lord.

To my Launch Team—Deep breath. Here we are. Thank you for being FOR this, for me—for Him. Thank you from the bottom of my heart for every way you were all of these things and for every way in which you shared in the joy of this study.

To Carolyn O'Neal—Thank you for loving women, for loving me and my family well, and for believing in God's work in me.

To Pastor Gregg and Kelly, Chad Overton, Adam Mason, David Wells, and my Houston's First Baptist Church Family—Thank you for allowing me to serve with you and for your tremendous help and confidence in the Spirit's work in me.

To Meredyth Cann—Thank you for cheering me on, for being my friend and for answering all of my fashion questions with grace.

To Anita Carman and Inspire Women—Thank you for investing (financially and spiritually) towards my graduate degree in Christian counseling.

To Troy and Kelley Sikes—Your story in Week Five says it all.

To Neb Hayden—Thank you for the years you and your wife have dedicated to the ministry, for digging deep so that others could benefit and understand the Gospels even better.

To Gari Meacham, my friend and writing mentor—I have thanked the Lord over and over again for bringing us together. You've taught me volumes about what it means to be a Christian woman and writer for the kingdom. It's been such a gift to have you as a head cheerleader in my court.

To Amanda Stephens, my writing buddy—We started writing together in a creative writing class in college, and you've been a most enjoyable, loyal companion ever since (through so much more than writing!). Thank you for your consistent encouragement.

To Leslie Einhaus—We didn't get our start in a college class, but you could say we've been writing together since the crib. While other cousins spent the summers going through popsicles and watercolor paints, our grandparents could never keep up our notebook paper supply. Our hobby started something that has never burnt out of either of us, and I'm so glad.

To Cortney Gough—Thank you for your friendship, your innovative ideas represented here and continuing to spur me on with this project and in the faith.

To Sandie Montgomery—The foundation of most of my Bible knowledge was under your teaching in high school; the majority of the rest falls from my own time in the Word, which I can also trace back to your discipleship.

To Maci Barnett—my lifelong spiritual mentor and friend. My fervor for showing women the lavish love of Jesus had its beginning with you.

To all of my family and friends who prayed for this and who continue to pray hand in hand with me for God's truth to be etched on the hearts of women, THANK YOU.

Note to Leaders

Visit www.randallhouse.com and receive a free Leader's Guide for *Preoccupied with Promise*. Discover tools to aid you in leading your small group through a six-week study exploring the significance of focusing on God's promises to us. In this on-line resource you will find practical insights for group discussion and suggested extras for each week.

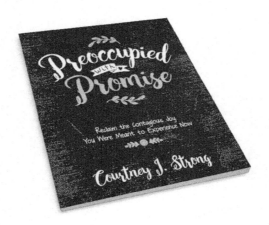

To order additional copies of *Preoccupied with Promise*
call 1-800-877-7030 or log onto www.randallhouse.com.
Call for quantity discounts.

Engraving Questions

_____
_____
_____
_____
_____
_____
_____
_____
_____
_____
_____
_____
_____
_____
_____

Endnotes

[1] Tenney, Merril C. (1995). John. In F.E. Gaebelein (Ed.), *The Expositor's Bible Commentary: With the New International Version: Vol. 5. John (p. 54)*. Grand Rapids, MI: Zondervan.

[2] Ibid, p. 54.

[3] Ibid, p. 55.

[4] Belk, Michael. *Journeys with the Messiah* (Santa Rosa Beach, FL: Journeys with the Messiah, 2009), p. 39.

[5] Zodhiates, Spiros, ThD., *The Complete Word Study Dictionary: New Testament*. (Chattanooga, TN: AMG Publishers) 1993. #225 p.120.

[6] Francis A. Schaeffer, *True Spirituality* (Carol Stream, IL: Tyndale House, 2001), p. 57.

[7] Barker, Kenneth L. and John R. Kohlenberger III (2004) *The Expositor's Bible Commentary - Abridged Edition: New Testament*. Grand Rapids, MI: Zondervan. Bible Gateway. Web. Accessed 29 Aug 2016.

[8] William Backus and Marie Chapian, *Telling Yourself the Truth* (Minneapolis, MN: Bethany House, 2000).

[9] Kendra Wilkinson, *Sliding into Home* (New York, NY: Gallery Books, 2010) 10.

[10] Robert S. McGee, *Father Hunger* (Robert S. McGee Publishing, 1993) 182.

[11] Cathy Lynn Grossman, "How Americans Imagine God," *USA Weekend*: 17-19 Dec. 2010: 7.

[12] Larry Crabb, *A Liberating Look at Gender: Releasing True Masculinity and True Femininity*, CO, NewWay Ministries, 2006. CD.

[13] Walsh, Bob. *Clear Blogging: How People Blogging Are Changing the World and How You Can Join Them* (Berkely, CA: Apress, 2007), p. 328.

[14] *Life Application Study Bible*. (Wheaton, IL: Tyndale House, 1991). 1784.

[15] Dave Busby, *Going off the Deep End*, (Maple Grove, MN: Dave Busby Ministries, 1993) p. 54.

[16] Francis A. Schaeffer, *True Spirituality* (Carol Stream, IL: Tyndale House, 2001), p. 56.

[17] Ibid, p. 55.

[18] Siegel, Daniel, M.D. Video Clip: Lifespan Learning Institute. Web Instructional Video. Viewed Mar. 2012. http://lifespanlearn.org.

[19] Fonagy, Peter, PhD FBA. "Attachment, Empathy and the Developmental Roots of Faith." 2010 Institute for Spirituality and Health. Texas Medical Center, Houston, TX 9 Nov. 2010.

[20] Ibid.

[21] Dave Busby, *Going off the Deep End*, (Maple Grove, MN: Dave Busby Ministries, 1993) p. 64-65.

[22] Ibid, pp. 73-74, reprinted with permission from Lawanna Busby St. Clair.

[23] Henry, Matthew. *Matthew.* N.p. 1706. *Matthew Henry Commentary on the Whole Bible (Complete)*. Bible Study Tools Online. Web. Accessed 8 Jun. 2012.

[24] W. Wiersby, "Crippled Daughter" from *Wycliffe Handbook of Preaching and Preachers* Copyright © 2006 Biblical Studies Press, reprinted with permission from http://bible.org

[25] Nancy Guthrie. *Abundant Life Day Book: 365 Blessings to Begin Your Day.* (Carol Stream: IL: Tyndale House Publishers, Inc., 2011), p. 314, November 10.

[26] *Measuring Mentalization* (Baron-Cohen et al., 2001) "Reading the Mind in the Eyes Test," as cited from Fonagy, Peter, PhD FBA. "Attachment, Empathy and the Developmental Roots of Faith." 2010 Institute for Spirituality and Health. Texas Medical Center, Houston, TX 9 Nov. 2010.

What is D6?

BASED ON DEUTERONOMY 6:4-7

A **conference** for your entire **team**

A **curriculum** for every age at **church**

An **experience** for every person in your **home**

Connecting
CHURCH & HOME
These must work together!

D6 CONFERENCE ONCE A YEAR

DEFINE & REFINE Your Discipleship Plan

www.d6family.com

ONE HOUR A WEEK

POWER OF PARENTAL INFLUENCE

CPSIA information can be obtained
at www.ICGtesting.com
Printed in the USA
LVOW04s2330050417
529790LV00001B/1/P